Testimonials

As Michael Roberts breathes fresh life into the timeless wisdom of John Wesley, we gain a valuable reminder of the importance of the Sermon on the Mount. This book will deepen your commitment to Jesus and show you how to live the radically blessed life God intends.

Magrey R. deVega,
Pastor and author of *Questions Jesus Asked* and *The Bible Year,* among other resources

John Wesley was known for speaking 'plain speech' for 'plain people,' and yet anyone who has read his standard sermons might be left wondering, "What is plain about this?" Through these paraphrases, Michael Roberts, along with Lauren DeLano Grosskopf, truly makes Wesley's own words 'plain' for us to better understand today. And it doesn't stop there. Through reflections, discussion questions, and devotions, Methodists can reconnect to these sermons in a new and revived way.

Ashley Boggan
General Secretary of the General Commission on Archives and History and author of *Wesleyan Vile-tality: Reclaiming the Heart of Methodist Identity,* among other books

Radically Blessed is a brilliant re-imagination of John Wesley's most powerful sermons for today's churchgoers. Through paraphrasing, devotions, and questions for reflection, Michael Roberts expertly curates thirteen of John Wesley's Standard Sermons, rendering Ordinary Time a season of deep insight and renewal. Together with Wesley, Roberts courageously tackles topics such as love of neighbor, politics, and the lies society tells. It is a must-read for disciples and apostles everywhere.

Rebekah Simon-Peter
Author of *Believe Like Jesus* and Founder of *Creating a Culture of Renewal*

As a Methodist pastor, I find the words of our founder, John Wesley, powerful and inspirational. This book does the heavy lifting and takes the sometimes difficult-to-decipher writings of this 18th-century theologian and reintroduces them to new generations in a way that is accessible, relevant, and applicable.

Matt Miofsky
Pastor and author of *The Methodist Book of Daily Prayer,* among other resources

Michael Roberts is an insightful pastor and leader who I deeply appreciate. This work, which draws from Wesley's message to illuminate the seasons of the church year, is a gift to us all.

Adam Hamilton
Pastor and author of *The Message of Jesus,* among many other books

Michael Roberts and Lauren Delano-Grosskopf have opened the wisdom of Wesley's sermons to a modern audience. Christ's invitation to covenant love and discipleship speaks with a fresh and powerful voice through this writing.

Bishop Laura Merrill
Arkansas, Oklahoma, and Oklahoma Indian Missionary Conferences of The United Methodist Church

Radically Blessed is a great book that I highly recommend for personal or small-group study in any local church. Every lay and clergy person would benefit from reading this book to get a better sense of John Wesley's theology. Like the first book in the series, this book leaves us wanting more and is a gift to our churches. I feel simply blessed through the reading of this book!

Bishop Bob Farr
Missouri Annual Conference of the United Methodist Church

What a quintessentially Wesleyan project! Roberts and Grosskopf offer lively paraphrases of Wesley's sermons, just as Wesley edited and paraphrased writings from his Anglican tradition. Like Wesley, they extend the themes of the paraphrases, offering their compelling sermons for contemporary life. This is an excellent resource for congregations and for pastors as a treasure trove for preaching. This series brings Wesleyan theology to life for our time, offering "plain truth for plain people."

Rebekah Miles
Susanna Wesley Centennial Professor of Practical Theology and Ethics, Perkins School of Theology, Southern Methodist University

I had the gift of getting to know Michael Roberts during the Academy for Spiritual Formation, and have deep gratitude for the authentic and genuine way he leads and writes for the church. This book, *Radically Blessed,* is an incredible resource for the church in this moment; these fresh paraphrases of Wesley's sermons open up easy connections between Jesus' teaching, Wesley's 18th-century wisdom, and this moment. At a time when the Christian church is navigating through conflicting, loud, and dangerous theologies, these reflections on the Sermon on the Mount are a ballast and a balm, offering persistent and consistent reminders of just how wild and beautiful the gospel message is.

Molly Vetter
Pastor and Retreat Leader for the upcoming Forty-Third Two-Year Academy for Spiritual Formation

With this series, two tasks are accomplished at once. First, excellent and easily accessible paraphrases are given of some of John Wesley's' most important sermons. Then, the authors expand on Wesley's thoughts with messages and reflections that are helpful for people today. A series like this has been needed for a long time.

David Livington
Pastor and author of *Getting to Good: Moving Towards a Fuller, More Abundant Life Right Now*

In *Radically Blessed,* Michael Roberts and his clergy colleague Lauren Delano Grosskopf once again bring John Wesley's timeless wisdom to life, making his 18th-century sermons on Jesus' Sermon on the Mount accessible and relevant for today's 21st-century church. The sermon paraphrases in this book capture Wesley's depth and passion in an incredible way, speaking powerfully to modern readers. What makes Radically Blessed a must-have is the addition of devotions and reflections for each sermon. These resources deepen the experience, especially for small groups, providing practical ways to apply Wesley's insights to daily life. Rooted in the Methodist spirit of transformation and renewal, this book invites readers to climb the mountain with Jesus, see the world through the lens of God's blessing, and embrace the radical call of discipleship.

Blake Bradford
Pastor and co-author of *Mission Possible 3* and *Mission Possible for the Small Church*

Radically Blessed is a much-needed book for Methodists. The depth of the devotions, coupled with an explanation of John Wesley's sermons, gives the reader insight into Wesley's message. The book also challenges the reader to reflect on their understanding of Jesus in the Gospels, who provokes people to act justly and live out the commandments of God. This book will be an excellent tool for both new and seasoned followers of John Wesley's teachings.

Natasha Murray
Pastor and District Superintendent, Arkansas Conference

Our Covenant group read Michael's book *Wanting More: Advent, Christmas, and Epiphany* during Advent and Epiphany. It was a great guide for our weekly chats and showed us how John Wesley's sermons are still relevant today. With Michael as a companion traveler on a spiritual formation journey, we are excited for his next book, *Radically Blessed*.

Khris Ford, Co-Director North Carolina Institute for Spiritual Direction

Susan Newton Graebe, NCCUMC, Coordinator of Residency in Ordained Ministry

Debora R Murphy, Fairway District Lay Leader

Pam Landreth Strug, Fairway District Director of Lay Servant Ministries

Claire Cox-Woodlief, Executive Director, White Memorial Presbyterian Church & CEO of CCW Transformation Ministries

Testimonials for *Wanting More,* the Previous Book in this Series

If you are looking for a resource to deepen your experience of God's love, you have found the right book. There is much to like about *Wanting More*. This book breathes new life into John Wesley's standard sermons by realigning them with Advent, Christmas, and Epiphany seasons. The abbreviation and modernization of the texts provide insight for a time such as this. Incisive questions accompanying each chapter make this book perfect for small group discussion and discipling. I find this book to be profoundly biblical, pastoral, and spiritually uplifting.

Paul W. Chilcote
Author of Multiplying Love: A Vision of United Methodist Life Together, among other resources

Rev. Dr. Michael Roberts is a pre-eminent voice in understanding John Wesley and making Wesley come alive for us today. A study like this one is needed in a season of our church's history when centering down on who we are is so valuable. I am grateful for this study.

Michelle Morris
Pastor and Author of *Gospel Discipleship: Four Pathways for Christian Disciples*

This book will take you on a treasure hunt! As a United Methodist, I've recently become passionate about looking back at our spiritual gems in order to move forward. I was delighted to discover that Michael Roberts is, too. Roberts selects and arranges Wesley's best sermons brilliantly, using plain language that is thematically relevant for the holidays. As he says about grace in the second chapter: "You do not want to miss this adventure." You truly don't. Read this book.

Stephen P. West
Pastor and author of *Something Happens Here: Reclaiming the Distinctiveness of Wesley's Communion Spirituality in Times of Divisiveness*

Radically Blessed

The Core Teachings of Jesus Through the Sermons of John Wesley

MICHAEL ROBERTS

WITH LAUREN DELANO GROSSKOPF

Market Square

Radically Blessed
The Core Teachings of Jesus through the Sermons of John Wesley

©2025 Michael Roberts

books@marketsquarebooks.com
141 N. Martinwood, Suite 2 Knoxville, Tennessee 37923

ISBN: 978-1-950899-91-3

Printed and Bound in the United States of America
Cover Illustration & Book Design ©2025 Market Square Publishing, LLC

Editor: Sheri Carder Hood
Cover Design: Kevin Slimp
Page Design: Ashley Connor
Post-Process Editor: Ken Rochelle

All rights reserved. No part of this book may be reproduced in any manner without written permission except in the case of brief quotations included in critical articles and reviews. For information, please contact Market Square Publishing, LLC.

Scripture quotations used with permission from:

NRSVUE
The New Revised Standard Version Updated Edition.
Copyright © 2021 National Council of Churches of Christ in the United States of America.
Used by permission. All rights reserved worldwide.

Contents

Introduction 1
From the Mountaintop

Chapter One 5
"Blessed are the Poor in Spirit and Those Who Mourn"
Sermon 21 in the Standard Sermons of John Wesley

Chapter Two 17
"Blessed are the Meek, the Merciful, and Those
Who Hunger for Righteousness"
Sermon 22 in the Standard Sermons of John Wesley

Chapter Three 27
"On Love"
Sermon 22 in the Standard Sermons of John Wesley, Part 2

Chapter Four 39
"Blessed are the Pure in Heart, the Peacemaker,
and the Persecuted"
Sermon 23 in the Standard Sermons of John Wesley

Chapter Five 51
"Salt and Light"
Sermon 24 in the Standard Sermons of John Wesley

Chapter Six 61
"The Fulfillment of the Law"
Sermon 25 in the Standard Sermons of John Wesley

Chapter Seven 71
"The Lord's Prayer"
Sermon 26 in the Standard Sermons of John Wesley

Chapter Eight 83
"On Fasting" (and modeling the middle way)
Sermon 27 in the Standard Sermons of John Wesley

Chapter Nine 95
"Treasures in Heaven"
Sermon 28 in the Standard Sermons of John Wesley

Chapter Ten 105
"Seek First the Kingdom of God"
Sermon 29 in the Standard Sermons of John Wesley

Chapter Eleven 115
"The Golden Rule"
Sermon 30 in the Standard Sermons of John Wesley

Chapter Twelve 125
"The Narrow Way"
Sermon 31 in the Standard Sermons of John Wesley

Chapter Thirteen 135
"True and False Prophets, Good and Evil Fruit"
Sermon 32 in the Standard Sermons of John Wesley

Chapter Fourteen 145
"Building on Solid Rock"
Sermon 33 in the Standard Sermons of John Wesley

About the Authors 155

Endnotes 157

A note about each chapter

This book is the second in a series where each chapter paraphrases one of Wesley's sermons, followed by a devotion on the same theme and questions for reflection.

INTRODUCTION

From the Mountaintop

For people called Methodists, the Sermon on the Mount is a big deal. Of the forty-four Standard Sermons of John Wesley, thirteen of these sermons are devoted to the core teachings of Jesus found in only three chapters of the Bible. That's about 30 percent. As Wesley says, "There is nothing else like this sermon in the whole of the scriptures, with the possible exception of the Ten Commandments." This sermon from Jesus lays out the "wisdom of God" and reveals the core dimensions of how we are to live in relationship with God. As we go through the Sermon on the Mount, we will be inspired by what it means to be merciful, to be the light of the world, to seek first the kingdom of God, and to build our home upon the rock rather than sand. There is so much here!

From the beginning, the Methodist movement has been one of optimism.[1] Starting with Wesley's consistent proclamation, we Methodists have emphasized salvation as a present reality and that we can truly be transformed to reflect the image of God in this world.[2] Transformation is the key! At every turn in his Sermon on the Mount, Jesus illustrates that God's ways are not our ways. We are being blessed—and that's a key word—to be a part of something counter-cultural and holy. Drawing upon the core teachings of Jesus, we are empowered to be peacemakers rather than mere peacekeepers. We are called to meekness, meaning we are to take the risk of opening our hearts to others with a love that is patient and kind and humble enough not to insist on its own way.[3] If we associate meekness with weakness, there is nothing meek about it. Another word for this way of being in the world is "holiness."

To help equip others for this way of life, Wesley published sermons and commended them to others in the Methodist movement. In time, several of these sermons were designated as "The Standard Sermons" and became part of our doctrine as people called Methodists.[4] And yet, these sermons do not get the attention they deserve. One reason is their length and style. They are written in eighteenth-century English and are very long by contemporary standards.

This realization provided the initial motivation for this project. To make these sermons more accessible, I began to read and then paraphrase them. My goal was to produce a paraphrase of fifteen hundred words or less that would capture the key themes of the sermons without taking away the inspiration.

This exercise revealed another reason for our lack of engagement with these sermons. In their original configuration, these sermons do not fit naturally into our church's liturgical seasons. For example, there is no straightforward sermon for Christmas, Easter, or Pentecost. Most often, Wesley was the guest preacher or was preaching outside the parish context, even as he encouraged all Methodists to participate in their local parishes. This reality sparked the question: could these sermons be rearranged to align with the contemporary rhythms of the church? In other words, could they be organized to fit the seasons of the liturgical year? After reading these sermons and outlining the key theological themes, this possibility began to take shape.[5]

The strongest motivation to move forward with this project was the belief that these sermons continue to have great relevance. They continue to open up the scriptures and give insights into faithful, fruitful living. Through this process, I became more and more convicted that these sermons have the power to bring renewal to congregations and the church as a whole in this and every age.

This book is the second in a series where each chapter paraphrases one of Wesley's sermons, followed by a devotion on the same theme and questions for reflection. The first book is *Wanting More: Advent, Christmas, and Epiphany, Inspired by the teachings of John Wesley*. This book, *Radically Blessed*, is designed as the third in the series, with fourteen chapters on the core teachings of Jesus found in the Sermon on the Mount. In terms of the liturgical year, the series is designed for Ordinary Time, perhaps through the summer. The plan is for two more books, one for Lent, Easter, and Pentecost, and another on Keys to Spiritual Growth, also for Ordinary Time. In the first book, a more comprehensive introduction to Wesley's theology is found in his sermons.[6]

Wesley's calling was to take the "glad tidings of salvation" outside the walls of the church and communicate in ways that would be relevant and meaningful to those beyond the hallowed walls. In his words, Wesley "consented to be more vile." This was a big decision for him, and it transformed the movement. This spirit motivated this series. The hope is to bring the powerful and practical theology of John Wesley to life for us today.[7]

In its original formation, this project was part of a yearlong worship and discipleship series developed within First United Methodist Church, Conway, Arkansas. Reverend Lauren DeLano, a colleague and friend, served as the associate pastor, collaborated with sermon ideas, preached her sermons built upon this collaboration, and helped develop the resources used for reflection and study. Her shared love for Wesley and inspired gifts for ministry brought much energy to this project. By "conferencing" together, we experienced a hope that Wesley advocated for all: a holy conversation with others leads to greater insight and inspiration. We are not meant to lead alone.

In this particular series, the image of the mountain is important. When we call the sermon that Jesus preached the "Sermon on the Mount," we talk about more than where the sermon was preached. Throughout scripture, the mountain represents being closer to God. From the mountaintop, our imaginations are awakened, and we can envision our lives as instruments of God's blessings in the world. We are then inspired to be a part of all God wants to bless. From the mountaintop, we can see a better way.

May this be your experience as you join in this journey to explore these core teachings of Jesus through the lens of Wesley's expositions and interpretations. Again, 30 percent of the Standard Sermons are devoted to these three chapters of the Bible. For Wesley, this sermon from Jesus is a big deal. May you be inspired and transformed by these important teachings from Jesus and John Wesley.

Michael Roberts

CHAPTER ONE

"Blessed are the Poor in Spirit and Those Who Mourn"

Upon the Lord's Sermon on the Mount – Discourse 1

(A devotional paraphrase)

Sermon 21 in the Standard Sermons of John Wesley

Paraphrase of Wesley sermon

When Jesus saw the crowds, he went up the mountain, and after he sat down, his disciples came to him. And he began to speak and taught them, saying:

"Blessed are the poor in spirit, for theirs is the kingdom of heaven."

"Blessed are those who mourn, for they will be comforted."

Matthew 5:1-4 (NRSVUE)

After preaching the gospel throughout Galilee and healing many who were sick, it is natural that crowds would come. Seeing the multitudes, Jesus went up to the mountain and began to teach. Let us take note of who is teaching. It is the Lord of heaven and earth, the Creator of all. It is the eternal wisdom of God, the one whose mercy is over all God's works. It is the God of love who emptied Godself, taking the form of a servant. And what is Jesus teaching? He is illuminating the way of heaven, the way to everlasting life.

Next, note that Jesus is teaching the multitudes, not only the apostles. As hard as some of these teachings are, they are not just for the select few and not just for "super-disciples." They point to the way of life for all. Finally, in terms of preliminaries, we can observe how Jesus teaches. He gives a general view of the whole, a foundational view of the values of heaven through eight beatitudes, as they have come to be called. There is nothing else like it in the scriptures, except maybe the Ten Commandments. With amazing love, Jesus pronounces God's blessing upon the poor in spirit, the meek, the merciful, those who mourn, and those who hunger for righteousness. He reveals the deep longing of our souls.

In these eight sayings, Jesus lays out the sum of all true religion. Some commentators believe that these sayings illuminate stages of the Christian journey. Others argue that these sayings are for all in all times. I ask, "Do we have to choose?" These temperaments are needed for faithfulness—in all times. And yet, there is also a reason why "poverty of spirit" is listed first and proceeds, to some degree, to active peacemaking and the possibility of persecution.

Each of these sayings starts with the word "blessed." Another translation of the word is "happy," although Jesus is talking about more than temporal happiness. Temporal happiness depends on outward circumstances. When things are going well, we can be happy. When we are in pain, happiness is not possible. But Jesus uses the common word "blessed" to point to a more "substantial happiness," "a disposition of heart" that is possible for us in all circumstances. He speaks of spiritual happiness, perhaps related to joy or rejoicing, a gift of the spirit not dependent on circumstances. The word "blessed" also shocks us to realize that when we live in a life-giving relationship with God, we seek and find happiness in things very different from what the world proclaims will bring happiness.

The foundation of this blessedness or happiness is "poverty of spirit." It is easy to imagine that Jesus looked upon the crowd that day and noticed that most were not rich. This shared condition became a doorway to talk about spiritual matters. Some argue that the "poor in spirit" are "those who love poverty; those who are free from covetousness, from the love of money." From this perspective, many have thought it necessary to totally divest themselves and take vows of poverty. While this perspective is worthy of our pondering, I do not believe Jesus intends us to focus on one particular vice. "Love of money" is among "a thousand other roots of evil in the world." Here, Jesus is focusing on something much bigger. His words are intended to "lay a general foundation whereon the whole fabric of Christianity may be built."

The "poor in spirit" are the humble, those who know they do not have the spiritual resources within themselves to make life meaningful or to make a connection to eternity. Apart from God's grace, we are wretched and poor, miserable and blind. In this condition, we find ourselves seeking to build ourselves up with pride and haughtiness of spirit, with a thirst for esteem and honor. Envy, anger, and bitterness will appear "in ten thousand shapes." The recognition of this reality can be called a "first repentance." The humility discovered can help open the way to faith in Christ. This recognition, given by God, can help lead us to the very kingdom of heaven.

What is this kingdom? The Apostle Paul says the kingdom of God is "righteousness, and peace, and joy in the Holy Spirit" (Rom 14:17). First, the kingdom is righteousness. Righteousness is the life of God in the soul; it is the image of God stamped upon the heart. In a word, it is the love of God. Love illuminates all that is right and good. Next, the kingdom is peace. This peace is "that calm serenity of soul," whereby we know we are accepted in Christ and loved by him. Next, the inward kingdom implies "joy in the Holy Spirit." This joy is a gift. It is a "seal upon our hearts of the redemption which is in Jesus."

This blessed poverty is true and genuine humility. It is the inward knowledge that we are totally dependent on God for every good thought, word, and work. It brings a "loving shame," even for the sins we know God has forgiven, and a desire to grow in grace and advance in the love of God through our Lord Jesus Christ.

Perhaps there were those that day who stood in prosperity and were not moved. Knowing this triumphant state does not last for long, our Lord proceeds to the second beatitude: "Blessed are those who mourn, for they shall be comforted." We might imagine that this refers to the sorrow from worldly loss, but more is implied. Here, Jesus also speaks of those who "mourn after God." They have "tasted the joy unspeakable" but now "cannot see him through the dark cloud" of temptation and sin returned. Mourning the loss of this joy leads to comfort. God honors this cry with a "fresh manifestation of love." We discover, once again, that nothing in life or death can separate us from the love of God, through Christ Jesus our Lord" (Rom 8:35-39).

This whole process seems to foreshadow the words Jesus spoke to his apostles on the night before he gave himself up for us when he said that they would weep and lament but that their sorrow would ultimately turn to joy (John 16:19f). As the psalmist proclaims, "Weeping may linger for the night, but joy comes with the morning" (Ps 30:5).

Another dimension of mourning needs to be mentioned. With Christ's love within, we find ourselves mourning for the sins and miseries of humankind. We weep with those who weep. Our hearts are opened to the hurts of the world. Yes, blessed are those who mourn, for this opens us to the very love of Christ, who wants to bring comfort, even through us.

To conclude our thoughts on these first two beatitudes, we remember how the Apostle Paul says that the wisdom of God is foolishness to the world. All this talk of poverty of spirit and mourning seems to be downright lunacy. Some might say having this much religion has made you crazy. But, for those whose eyes are enlightened, we are able to see the light of love in these sayings and know that this is what is real, even unto eternity itself. In this light, we cry out. We weep until Christ wipes away the tears. We weep for the miseries that fill this earth and trust the day will come when our poverty in spirit will be redeemed into "the immeasurable riches of God's grace" (Eph 2:7). In Christ, the blessings of God shall cover the earth as the water covers the sea.

Amen.

"Blessed are ..."

Matthew 5:1-4

Pastor Lauren, whose name you'll also find on the cover of this book, researched and discovered that the social media hashtag "#blessed" is used, on average, five hundred times an hour. Now, if you aren't on social media and don't know what that means, just know this: the word "blessed" is used a lot to describe how we feel. It is most often used when people have achieved or accomplished something. A quick search of the word "blessed" last week led us to an athlete being blessed by scoring a thousand points in their college basketball career, then to someone getting a promotion, and finally, to a parent who was blessed that their kids woke up and dressed for school all by themselves. This is not all bad. It is good to feel a sense of God's love and favor upon you. Sometimes, however, we can get pretty selfish about it and start thinking that God is there to fulfill our personal desires and give us what we think will make us happy. When we fall into this temptation, it is good to step back and ask: is that what Jesus has in mind when he uses the word "blessed"?

To answer this question, perhaps the best place to turn is to the Sermon on the Mount. This sermon marks the beginning of Jesus' public ministry in the Gospel of Matthew. After calling his disciples and healing many, the crowds increased. We can picture it. Many had gathered, and Jesus wanted to teach them and share the ways of heaven with them. He went up to the mountain so everyone could hear, and then he laid out the foundation for what Wesley called "true religion." We will explore the whole Sermon on the Mount during this series, but for the next three weeks, we will specifically look at the eight blessings that start this sermon. We call these blessings the Beatitudes.

Each saying begins with the words "Blessed are." Another translation you may have heard is "Happy are." The original Greek word *Makarios* can be translated both ways. The prefix "mak" means to "extend" or "enlarge." The second part of the word suggests fortune, benefits, or advantage. Jesus and the scriptures combine the common word "blessed" with descriptions that shock us into a new perspective. We learn that God's ways are not our ways.

If we translate "blessed" as happy, we must remember that this happiness is much more than the happiness the world proclaims. Like with the term "blessed," Jesus has something more in mind. What the world says will bring happiness is not the same kind of happiness that comes when we live in a life-giving relationship with God. What the world says is blessed differs greatly from what God wants to bless.

We are so used to hearing sayings like these: "Blessed (or happy) are those who have it all together," "Blessed (or happy) are those who are sure of themselves," "Blessed (or happy) are those who have the good life." We envy them. We want what they have. But Jesus says something very different: blessed are those who know they can't make it on their own, who need help, who are meek, merciful, who hunger and thirst not for "things" but for God. In his Sermon on the Mount, Jesus shocks us with these blessings by turning our attitudes and expectations upside down.

These blessings come as we are willing to see things from a totally different perspective. These blessings are radical in the sense of being central, fundamental, and absolutely necessary for the life God wants for us—a life that is abundant, blessed, and eternal.

This sermon from Jesus starts with, "Blessed are the poor in spirit, for theirs is the kin-dom of heaven." Are you shocked by this? We are so used to thinking that the blessed are the smartest, richest, best-looking, most privileged, or most advantaged. The blessed are those who "have," and those who "don't have" are not as blessed. This perspective is part of the so-called "prosperity gospel," which proclaims that God blesses and rewards us with success and wealth when we work hard, give in faith, and live a good life. Jesus' first blessing, however, is to the poor in spirit. He wants us to know that we are all poor in this way. None of us has the spiritual resources within us to make life meaningful or to connect to eternity. We don't have the means to buy this.

From this disposition of poverty, a great promise is given: "Blessed are the poor in spirit, for theirs is the kin-dom of heaven." Our lives are opened to the "immeasurable riches of God's grace" (Eph 2:7). These riches do not come from within us. They come in relationship with our living God. That's the blessing.

Note we will use the term "kin-dom" in our sermons and devotions and "kingdom" in the paraphrases. Both "kin-dom" and "kingdom" are translations of the Greek word that points to a way society is organized. The newer translation, "kin-dom," which focuses on kin or family, may come closer to what Jesus is trying to reveal here.

With either translation, Jesus is teaching that God's way of organizing relationship differs from the ways of the world. Perhaps this newer translation can help us see this more clearly or at least give us a new perspective.

To illuminate this first beatitude, I draw from the underlying message of Alcoholics Anonymous, whereby participants admit they are powerless over their lives and turn their lives over to a power greater than themselves. Blessed are those who know they are in need, for they are able to receive God's blessings, God's grace, and God's gifts.

In the next beatitude, Jesus further shakes up our worldly understanding of blessing and happiness by saying, "Blessed are those who mourn, for they shall be comforted." In John Wesley's sermon, which inspires us today, he makes it clear that Jesus is calling us to expand our understanding of mourning and grieving beyond conventional thoughts. We typically think of grieving the loss of a loved one. God is certainly with us in such grief, but here, Jesus directs us to open our hearts to a deeper understanding. As we open our hearts to the love of God, our hardened hearts are softened, and we begin to experience a sense of spiritual grief for all the pain in the world. Our hearts break when we notice children going hungry, for example. We grieve when we see human beings violated by selfish greed or deep-seated prejudices that cause so much harm. In God's providence, this grief is a blessing. It leads to comfort and our wanting to be a source of God's comfort.

The word "comfort" is rich with meaning. To comfort is to come alongside, walk with another, and be present and supported. It is such a blessing! In our spiritual grief, God comes alongside us and walks with us. We know that we are not alone and that joy will come. God will redeem the grief of the world. In addition—and this is big—we are empowered to be this comfort for others. We are called to be those who come alongside others and be the presence of God.

As we study the Beatitudes, we must consider what these blessings mean for our lives today. As people of faith, we live in this state of "already but not yet." The reign of God has come and is revealed to us as Jesus heals, eats with sinners, and proclaims the presence of God's kin-dom, and yet we know that this world is not yet fully reflective of this kin-dom on earth as it is in heaven. And so, we pray for that kin-dom every day. We embrace the calling to open our hearts to God and soften our hearts to God's love. We let this love in, and it creates within us a divine mixture of joy and sorrow all at the same time. We know God's love, and we grieve knowing how far our world is from this love. We want to close the gap. We want the world to be truly blessed. That's what Jesus wants for all of us. As we go on this journey together into the Sermon on the Mount, may we all be truly blessed.

Amen.

Reflections for Devotion and Discipling

1. Why does Wesley devote much time to Jesus' teachings in the Sermon on the Mount? Who is meant to be the recipient of this teaching?

As mentioned in the introduction, 30 percent of Wesley's Standard Sermons are devoted to the three chapters of the Bible that contain what we call the Sermon on the Mount. For Wesley, these core teachings of Jesus give us the "eternal wisdom of God." And make no mistake about it: this wisdom is counterculture. This wisdom provides an alternative way of viewing reality, and it is challenging. We cannot live into this reality alone—without God or each other. And that is among the main points. From the beginning, we note that these teachings are not for the few or for "super-disciples" but for all. These teachings provide a map into the true and abundant life that God wants for all of us.

2. What does it mean to be "blessed"?

Wesley says that the sum of all true religion can be found in these eight key sayings that start with the word "blessed." This word is sometimes translated as "happy." Wesley used both terms but seems to favor the latter. The word "happy," as we tend to use it, suggests a feeling produced by something outside ourselves. Happiness depends on the circumstances around us. Jesus likely had something different in mind, perhaps something like the fruit of the spirit named "joy." This gift transcends circumstances and is guarded from the ways of the world. The translation "blessed" has similar issues. This word is used to suggest God's special favor or fortune. From the context of the Sermon on the Mount, blessings are found in something other than what the world promotes. While we fully acknowledge that God loves all, we discover here that this deeper blessing is reserved for those willing to "repent and believe," as Jesus said earlier. This deeper blessing comes as we cultivate God's values and God's will into our lives.

3. What does it mean to be "poor in spirit?" How can we know this blessing? What is the outcome of this blessing?

   The first sermon in this series deals with the first two beatitudes. The first and, thus, the foundational blessing comes to those who are "poor in spirit." Review the definitions and interpretations found in Wesley's sermon and our devotion.

4. Why does Jesus say we are blessed when we mourn? What is the promise that comes with this blessing?

   Once again, the world would say something very different. All this talk of poverty and mourning sounds foolish to our worldly ears. In the Sermon on the Mount, Jesus shocks us with these blessings by turning our attitudes and expectations upside down. These blessings come as we are willing to see things from a totally different perspective.

CHAPTER TWO

"Blessed are the Meek, the Merciful, and Those Who Hunger for Righteousness"

Upon the Lord's Sermon on the Mount – Discourse 2

(A devotional paraphrase)

Sermon 22 in the Standard Sermons of John Wesley

Paraphrase of Wesley sermon

"Blessed are the meek, for they will inherit the earth."

"Blessed are those who hunger and thirst for righteousness, for they will be filled."

"Blessed are the merciful, for they will receive mercy."

Matthew 5:5-7

"Blessed are the meek!" There are some misconceptions around the word "meek." The meek are not the ignorant or those who do not know what is happening. The meek are not the innocent, those who are sheltered from the shocks of life and are thus naïve. The meek are not the docile or passive, perhaps too scared to act for good in the world. Ignorance, innocence, and apathy are as far from meekness as from true humanity. Meekness implies a softness of heart that is open to others. This temperament resists the fear that causes us to build walls and harden our hearts. Meekness takes great courage.

With that said, there is a sense of resignation within the term "meekness." As Jesus speaks of it, meekness is a calm acquiescence to God's will for us. The meek can say, "Not my will, but yours be done." The meek turn it all over to God. Meekness does not imply being without zeal for God, but this zeal is tempered with love, which is always patient, kind, and gentle, never insisting on its own way or trying to force others into it.

Meekness not only restrains outward acts of harm but tempers inward dispositions as well. The opposite of meekness is when our hearts judge, condemn, and try to fix others from a spirit of arrogance and self-righteousness. While the meek shall inherit the earth, this personal assertiveness and hubris take away what we think we deserve.

Later in the same chapter of Matthew, Jesus uses some extreme examples to make this point. He compares the commandment "you shall not kill" to being angry in our hearts. Even with this inward sin, we are still in danger of the same judgment as one who acts outwardly in the eyes of God. Our inheritance is at risk. Jesus then speaks of Gehenna's judgment for those who hold any unkindness in their hearts or think of others as fools. Gehenna—where the image of hell comes from—was the continuously burning trash pit outside the city. The original hearers would have had a tough time making the connection between these seemingly innocent judgments and being thrown into the fire. The point is that we all fall short. We are all in need of grace! To forget this is to become "obnoxious," which means to cause harm. We take away the blessings of the earth, which we all share. We take away the blessings of living together. To do this well, meekness is needed. We can also use other descriptive words: humble, submissive, gentle, patient, and seeing good in others. The world might call such temperament foolish; God calls them blessed.

The next beatitude is this: "Blessed are those who hunger and thirst for righteousness." Hunger and thirst are the strongest of all appetites. If these cravings are not fulfilled, nothing can take their place in our minds, and nothing can satisfy them but food and drink. Without them, we die.

The image of hunger and thirst points to the deepest longing of our souls. We want and need "righteousness," which enfolds every holy temperament into one. Righteousness is the sum of true religion—or true holiness—and is the only thing that will satisfy the hungry soul for God. What the world accounts for, religion will not do it. The religion of the world implies three things: doing no harm, doing good, and attending to the means of grace—at least going to church.

Following these rules may make one "religious," but they will not satisfy one who hungers for God or for righteousness. Deep within, we long for a religion much deeper and higher than these outward "forms of religion." We long for the knowledge of God in Christ Jesus. We long for the love, peace, and joy in the Holy Spirit, by which righteousness is defined (Rom 14:17). As we hunger and thirst for this, the promise is given; we shall be satisfied.

Next, Jesus says, "Blessed are the merciful for they shall obtain mercy." "Mercy" is another great word of faith. It is much more than leniency and much more than letting up on a display of power. That's how we often use the word, as if it is a weakness. For us, mercy is active love. In fact, it is much like the love described by the Apostle Paul in the thirteenth chapter of First Corinthians. This mercy is patient and kind, never insisting on its own way, always wanting what is good for the other. We may have all doctrines in order and have faith to move mountains, but without this mercy, we have nothing. This mercy inspires "the most fervent and tender affection." It is never rash or hasty in judgment. In mercy, we hold lightly what one person says against another and do not easily believe what we might say about ourselves either. In mercy, we respond with compassion, even for those who do not hunger after God. In mercy, we feed even our enemy when there is hunger and give that "cup of cold water" that might be able to melt the heart.

And the promise is given. The merciful will receive mercy. You may ask, "But when?" You may look out and say facetiously, "See how these Christians love one another!" with tears in your eyes. These Christians who are "tearing out each other's bowels, party against party, faction against faction, torn asunder with envy, jealousy, anger, and domestic strife ... these Christians who bear the name of Christ, the Prince of Peace, and wage continual war with each other, desiring only power in their hands"—how can we hide this, either from Jews, Muslims, or others among us? "What wrath, what contention, what malice, what bitterness is everywhere found among them, even where they agree in essentials and only differ in opinions or the circumstantials of religion! O God, how long must we wait?" Where is this promised mercy amid so much unmercifulness?

Our high and holy calling is to be part of the first fruits of God's kingdom coming to earth. May the Lord God fill our hearts with such a love for every soul that we may be ready to lay down our lives for the sake of another. May our souls continually overflow with love, swallowing up every unkind and unholy temperament until Christ calls us into the full reign of love forever and ever. By the power of the Holy Spirit working within us, be meek and merciful, always hungering and thirsting for righteousness. This is the way of true life. This is the way to know the mercy God has and wants for us all.

Amen.

Blessings that Fulfill (On Father's Day)

Matthew 5:5-7

As I write the words of this chapter, I'm reminded of a particular Fathers' Day. I remember getting home from work. I was tired and a little overwhelmed by it all. Dede was at a meeting, so I was responsible for feeding myself and three hungry children. I looked in the pantry and found a couple of cans of Chef Boyardee Ravioli—which wouldn't be enough—but then I noticed a can of SpaghettiOs and got the brilliant idea to combine them. Ravioli and Os, plus some buttered bread and green beans, and you've got what my now adult children called "the million-dollar meal." They loved it! A week later, I was gone for the night, and our children begged Dede to make the million-dollar meal. It was a flop.

I've reflected on that million-dollar meal many times

through the years, and I think I know what made my combination of Ravioli and SpaghettiOs so much better than DeDe's. While I talked about how good it would be in advance, I think the kids were mainly really hungry and anxious, thinking there might be nothing else with me in the kitchen. I believe that's what made it so good that night.

Hunger makes all the difference in the world. If you are hungry, food tastes so much better. If you are in a circumstance where hunger is a true reality, then food becomes such a blessing. It is not something to take for granted, as many of us do. To fast occasionally, experiencing hunger and thirst opens our hearts to the power of thanksgiving and keeps us from taking this blessing for granted.

As Jesus proclaimed the ways of God to the crowd before him, he awakened a hunger and thirst they may not have even known they had. But as they heard Jesus' words, they became hungry for something more than food. I hope that has happened to you—and maybe is happening right now.

Jesus put a name to what we really need to live—and when I say "live," I don't mean just to exist but to live life out of the blessings of God. Blessed are those who hunger and thirst for "righteousness." That is the food of life, according to Jesus. In his sermon that inspires us today, John Wesley says that "righteousness" is the sum of true religion. Righteousness is the one thing that will satisfy the hungry soul. Righteousness is the spiritual version of steak and a loaded baked potato with a Caesar salad—or whatever your idea of a great meal might be.

So, what is this righteousness? True righteousness is

a "right relationship" with God, where our life is aligned with God's love, and we are able to live by the virtues of God's kin-dom. These virtues are often named in the scriptures: patience, kindness, humility, and compassion. Righteousness is a life that bears others up in love. Righteousness is the blessing that will truly satisfy the hungry heart.

John Wesley helps us see this distinction. As Jesus did so many times, he points out that true religion or true righteousness is not rooted in "outward forms of faith." Too many people think to be religious is to look good on the outside. Do a few good things. Go to church. Give. Then maybe you'll receive a blessing or at least avoid God's wrath. That's the sum of religion for many. Later in the gospel, Jesus compares this superficial religiosity to being like a painted tomb—beautiful on the outside but dead inside. That's not what God wants for us. Deep in our spirits, we long for something more. We long for a right relationship with God where we can experience love, peace, and joy—not just to know about these things but to know them in our hearts. And God makes a promise: "Blessed are those who hunger and thirst for righteousness, for they shall be filled."

Wesley then says this: the more we are filled with the life of God, the more "tenderhearted" we become. That's his word. We become less judgmental and impatient and condemning of others. We learn true righteousness, leading us to the other blessings surrounding this beatitude. We might think of this as a "righteousness sandwich," with the bread around the meat being meekness and mercy. Three blessings, with righteousness in the middle.

First meekness. Jesus says, "Blessed are the meek."

Some may think of meekness as being weak, docile, or detached. It is not. Meekness is true strength. The meek trust that God is at work and always abounds in patience, kindness, and steadfast love. Therefore, the meek do not believe they have to defend God. It is not their job to judge and divide. The meek listen. The meek work to build relationships. There is nothing weak about meekness.

Next is mercy. We read, "Blessed are the merciful, for they shall receive mercy." Mercy can also be portrayed as weakness, but not for Jesus. Mercy is active love, always willing to forgive and cultivate relationships that work toward new life, new opportunities, and new beginnings. I love this sentence from Wesley: "In mercy, it is possible for us to say, 'I am so far from lightly believing what one person says against another, that I will not easily believe what one says against themselves. I will always allow second thoughts, and many times counsel too.'"

Then we are given a promise: "The merciful shall receive mercy." You may wonder about that. It sometimes seems that the merciful get run over, even by other so-called Christians. In this regard, John Wesley speaks of Christians who thrive on the judgment of others, drawing hard lines in the sand and making all kinds of ultimatums about what others should believe and do. It is so easy for us to get caught up in that kind of superficial self-righteousness. From God's perspective, however, it may be that those who judge will receive judgment. That may be the corresponding truth to what Jesus says here. Show mercy, and, at least from God, you will receive mercy.

So, those are the three beatitudes we are focusing on today. I hope you will put these blessings into practice, for that's when they truly come to life and open up the way of God. Open your heart to mercy and meekness. Open your heart to the fruits of true righteousness, to true strength. May you receive the goodness of God that truly satisfies.

Amen.

Reflections for Devotion and Discipling

1. What does it mean to "hunger and thirst for righteousness"? What is the promise associated with this blessing?

   In these blessings, Jesus wants to awaken a hunger in us that we may not even know we had. Jesus puts a name to it: "righteousness." Righteousness is the food of life, according to Jesus. Review this sermon and reflect upon what righteousness is and is not. In Wesley's sermon on this blessing, righteousness is called the "sum of true religion."

2. How might we characterize our deepest longings? What do we really want?

   Elsewhere, Wesley gives us a set of "general rules" for Christian community: do no harm, do good, and attend to the means of grace—worship, prayer, reading scripture, and the like. He commends these rules as absolutely necessary for faithfulness and fruitfulness. These means of grace even relate to how the name "Methodist" came about. Thus, it is worth noting that, in this sermon, Wesley talks about these rules in a more negative light. He uses these rules to show what the world sees as religion. Following these rules may make us "religious" but will not satisfy our deeper hunger and thirst. According to the Apostle Paul, the kingdom of God is not found in food or drink or any "outward form of religion" but in righteousness, love, peace, and joy in the Holy Spirit. The desire for these blessings calls us into a personal relationship. Religion is much more than following rules and affirming doctrine.

3. What does it mean to be "meek?" What is the promise associated with this blessing?

"Meekness" is not a word we use much today. Some translations use the word "humble." Note the similarities between "humble" and "human." To be humble or meek is to know that we are not God. Thus, it is not our job to judge or fix according to our wisdom. The meek listen. The meek find ways to see others as human beings worthy of love. By the world's standards, meekness can be considered a weakness. In God's providence, meekness reveals true strength. The powerful of the world try to take all that the earth provides. Here, we discover that all the blessings of life will ultimately be given to the humble at heart. Once again, God turns the values of the world upside down.

4. What does it mean to be "merciful"? What is the promise associated with this blessing?

Mercy is much more than leniency or even forgiveness. Mercy calls us to actively work for new life in relationships. In the original language, the word is akin to "womb," a place of new life. In Wesley's sermon here, he launches into what might be described as a whole other sermon on love, using 1 Corinthians 13 as his text. (We will explore this more in the next chapter). What is the connection between mercy and love? Also, note Wesley's strong admonition to the church that fails to practice this mercy and love.

CHAPTER THREE

"On Love"

(A devotional paraphrase)

Sermon 22 in the Standard Sermons of John Wesley, Part 2

Paraphrase of Wesley sermon

(Wesley's written sermons were often much longer than those delivered. They are meant to be teaching resources. This paraphrase is taken from the second sermon in Wesley's series on the Sermon on the Mount, where Wesley launches into what we might call a whole new sermon on "love." Wesley offers similar expositions of 1 Corinthians 13 in other sermons as well).

> *If I speak in the tongues of humans and of angels but do not have love, I am a noisy gong or a clanging cymbal. And if I have prophetic powers and understand all mysteries and all knowledge and if I have all faith so as to remove mountains but do not have love, I am nothing. If I give away all my possessions and if I hand over my body so that I may boast[a] but do not have love, I gain nothing.*
>
> *Love is patient; love is kind; love is not envious or boastful or arrogant or rude. It does not insist on its own way; it is not irritable; it keeps no record of wrongs; it does not rejoice in wrongdoing but rejoices in the truth It bears all things, believes all things, hopes all things, endures all things.*
>
> *Love never ends. But as for prophecies, they will come to an end; as for tongues, they will cease; as for knowledge, it will come to an end.*
>
> 1 Corinthians 13:1-8

How often do we see Christians tearing each other apart, party against party, faction against faction, torn asunder with envy and anger without end? How can we bear the name of the Prince of Peace and wage continual war with each other, as if drunk on the blood of the saints, convinced that we can control others? And yet, we wait in hope with patience. In Christ, the gospel has come and is coming, and the time will come when nation shall not lift up sword against nation, and we shall love one another as Christ has loved us.

We are called to be among the first fruits of this harvest. To do this, we must embrace the love of God planted deeply in our hearts and let it overflow into the world. The thirteenth chapter of 1 Corinthians is among the best places for us to turn in the scriptures for a comprehensive description of what this love looks like. Here, we learn how love can swallow up every unholy temperament and action. In this section of the written sermon, in the middle of a sermon on the Beatitudes, I want to give a full account of this grand theme of faith, which is at the heart of all true religion. The words of 1 Corinthians 13 help us put meekness and mercy into action.

First, love "suffers long," implying patience towards all. Love "suffers all the weakness, ignorance, errors, infirmities, and littleness of faith." It is even patient with the malice and wickedness found in the world. And this patience remains to the end, always feeding our enemy when there is hunger and giving that "cup of cold water" that might be able to melt the heart. That's merciful love, a love that brings life into the world.

This love is also "kind," working to overcome evil with

good. The word "kind" is not easily translated but is akin to soft, mild, and benign. Kindness is far from all "harshness of spirit" and softens our hardness of heart.

Consequently, "love is not envious." It is the direct opposite. Love wants all good things for every soul in this world and the world to come. Likewise, love is not "rash or hasty in judging." It will not hastily condemn anyone. True love weighs all the evidence—particularly brought in favor of the accused—and does not jump to conclusions.

In addition, love "is not puffed up." Love keeps us from thinking of ourselves more highly than we should. Knowing that we are not God or above others humbles us and makes us servants of all. Rather than divide, love binds us together with forgiveness, understanding, and compassion. Similarly, love is "not rude" or "willingly offensive to any." It honors all. A popular writer says that good breeding is found in politeness. If so, then none is so well-bred as a Christian, a lover of all humankind. This love seeks to "become all things to all people, that we might by all means save some" (1 Cor 9:22).

In doing this, love "never insists on its own way." This love does not let opinions and perspectives become the focus of relationships. We come together to learn how to love, forgive, honor, and bless one another, not to win arguments.

With all of this, it is worth noting that even the writer of these words, the Apostle Paul, had moments where he seemed to lack this love. One example would be his contention with Barnabas. The discord was so sharp that they split apart, with Barnabas and John going one way and Paul and Silas another. In this encounter, there was a "sharpness of anger." However, God used even this situation for good and for the spread of the gospel. Failure to practice this love does not lower the bar or the normative standard.

Love, described in this way, does not mean we turn our backs on evil, trying to be meek and humble. If, for example, we see another strike a neighbor, we should intervene in love. At the same time, love prevents us from rushing to judgment. Too often, we are tempted to infer evil where it is not. Love can confront evil but does so without the quickness to believe evil. Love looks for the good and seeks ways to build bridges.

Love does not rejoice in sin, as common as it is even among those who bear the name of Christ. If we are too zealously attached to "any party," we are likely to gain pleasure in the fall of others. Only a person of love can avoid this perverse joy. Only a person of love can weep with an enemy.

Love "rejoices in the truth." And make no mistake about it: God's truth is revealed less in opinions and more in how we interact with one another. Truth brings forth holiness of heart and conversation, rejoicing that even those with different opinions or faith practices are lovers of God and bear good fruit in the world. God's relational truth is revealed not in like-mindedness or party zeal but in our learning to love one another. Love is truth and reveals God!

This love also "bears or covers all things." Let us not be that self-righteous person who thinks they have special permission to disapprove of others. That kind of witness only serves to dim the love of Christ and, most often, is a stumbling block at least equal to the act of which you disapprove. True love moves us away from making the faults and failures of others the topic of our conversations. Love reminds us that such back-biting, gossiping, and self-righteous whispering is to Christ the same as being a murderer.

Love "believes all things." Love is always willing to think the best and put the most favorable hope on everything. Love condemns as little as possible. It makes allowance for human weakness and works for good in relationship.

And when love cannot believe, love "hopes all things." Even when sin seems obvious, love compels us to search for another way to see and understand the circumstances. Love seeks to discern the heart behind actions. And even when "all actions and intentions are all clearly evil, even then love hopes that God will give victory and that there will be joy in heaven over this one sinner who repents, more than over ninety-nine just persons who need no repentance."

Lastly, love "endures all things"—not some things but all things. Whatever the injustice, the malice, and the cruelty humanity inflicts, love calls us to endure, to suffer all things through Christ who gives us strength. And this suffering does not destroy love. No! It is "a flame that burns even in the midst of the greatest darkness." It triumphs over all. It never fails, either in time or in eternity.

Once again, we have the honor of being among the first fruits of this harvest. Ask for this blessing. May your soul overflow with love, swallowing up every unkind and unholy temperament, until Christ calls you up into the reign of love, forever and ever.

Amen.

Practicing Politics AS the Church

Matthew 5:5-7; 1 Corinthians 13:1-8

In this sermon from John Wesley, he asks this haunting question: "How often do we see Christians tearing each other apart, party against party, faction against faction, torn asunder with envy and anger without end? How can we bear the name of the Prince of Peace and wage continual war with each other?" That's what happens when we take what is good and right and use that to divide and judge and harm others. That's what happens when we are "drunk with the blood of the saints." This powerful image suggests how we can easily take something good and abuse it.

Wesley is talking about politics. So yes, I am going to go there now. I don't blame you for being a little nervous. Talking about politics from the pulpit can be done so poorly. I guess the verdict is out on whether I can do any better. I will promise not to tell you how to vote. In fact, I hope you will not know exactly how I will vote in every election because I'm not even talking about politics out there. I'm talking about politics in the church. How do we practice politics AS the church?

When Wesley broaches this subject in his sermon, he does so in the context of a long discourse on the meaning of love. Wesley launches into a whole sermon on the meaning of love in the middle of his sermon on the Beatitudes. He talks about what it means to be humble and merciful, and then he says, in effect, We cannot understand any of that if we don't understand love. So, Wesley turns to 1 Corinthians 13 and launches into a long discourse on the meaning of love.

Wesley turned to these words often. We read that love is patient and kind. Love does not insist on its own way. Let that sink in. In love, we can never demand that others do things our way. To use a political term, we can say that love demands compromise. "Compromise" is not a popular word right now. For many, compromise is seen as caving in. It is seen as weakness. All too often in our world today, the goal is to win and even destroy the other side in the process. But that is not the way of love or the way of God. It is worth noting that the word "compromise" contains the word "promise." That's a good biblical word. The prefix "com" means "with" or "together." So, the compromise means to come together under a higher promise. Compromise seeks to understand first. It seeks common ground and searches for ways of doing things that might be better than the way of either side alone. That is the way of love.

Wesley talks about the problems of "party against party." The words "party," "partisan," and "partner" all share a common root: "part." We are all "part" of something bigger. We are "part" of a larger whole. For the whole to be healthy, we need people with diverse perspectives who offer different ideas. Differing perspectives help us see the whole more clearly and develop better solutions. It is dangerous when a "part" starts to think of themselves as the whole, as the sole owners of truth. That mindset exhibits the opposite of true love.

If I said that compromise was needed for a family to function in a healthy way, I suspect you would instantly agree. Compromise in our families is love in action. If I said this was true at work, I suspect you would agree. You may have heard a statement to the effect that, in a work environment, if two people have the same perspective on everything, one of them is unnecessary. Compromise is essential for creativity and productivity. And it is true for a larger community as well. We must meet in the middle, where, at the very least, we can learn how to love one another. Learning that is greater than any decision we might make.

All of this leads us to the word "communion," which speaks to the issue of practicing politics AS the church. Think about who Jesus invited into communion—fishermen and lawyers, tax collectors and prostitutes, rich and poor, Jews and Gentiles, men and women, and even children. Most of these invitations sparked controversy at the time. How dare Jesus invite them, but he did. And he invited all of them not only into a personal relationship with him but also into communion with one another. He invites us to be united—not in opinions but in the calling to practice love. John Wesley once said, "Though we may not all think alike, we can all love alike." We can practice politics in a way that leads to growth in love. That's our witness to the world as Christians.

There are churches where the pastor could stand and tell the congregation how to vote, and everyone would nod in agreement. We are called to give a different witness—a witness of coming together in great diversity with the common goal of learning how to love one another as Christ loves us. I pray we can keep that spirit in a world that is increasingly calling us to divide.

Politics is the art of making decisions for the good of the whole. By this definition, we practice politics every day—in our homes, at work, in the church, and as citizens. How do we do this well? There is only one way: to heed the call to love. It takes courage to do that. If you happen to encounter someone who is spewing vitriolic, hateful, disrespectful political speech, I hope you will have the courage to gently give voice to a different perspective, not necessarily on the issue at hand (you may agree with them on that), but on how we talk about the issue and interact with one another. That's where our higher calling comes in. May God help us all live into this higher witness as we engage one another in what seems to be a never-ending political season.

Amen.

Reflections for Devotion and Discipling

1. Re-read 1 Corinthians 13. What stands out for you? What challenges you?

    It has often been said that Wesleyan theology can be summed up in the word "grace." As a theological concept to describe how God responds to our sin, this is a good word. From the standpoint of practicing faith, however, Wesley uses the word "love" as much as ten times more often than he uses the word "grace." Love is the "royal law of heaven and earth," the one thing that endures forever, the sum of all the law and the prophets. Wesley outlines the thirteenth chapter of 1 Corinthians in several places within the sermons to define true love for us. With its frequent use, we can say 1 Corinthians 13 is a passage that serves as a lens through which Wesley interprets all scripture. This love is at the heart of our hermeneutic, or our system, for interpreting the whole. (For more on Wesley's hermeneutic, see the reflections in Chapter 4 of Wanting More, another book in this series.)

2. What does it mean to say that "love is patient and kind"?

We can be patient when we trust that God is at work in all, even in those who may see things differently than we do. In this same way, we can be kind. Kindness is akin to "softness" and is the opposite of "hardness of heart." In love, we avoid "hard thoughts" towards others and do not draw hard lines in the proverbial sand.

3. What does it mean to say that love is not hasty in judging and does not insist on its own way? What does this say about politics and how we practice politics AS the church?

Re-read what Wesley says about party against party, faction against faction. This is not the way of Christ. We are called to give witness to a higher way and have the honor of being among the first fruits of this harvest. As the body of Christ, we come together first to learn how to love one another. Our true witness is revealed in this love more than in our agreement on any issue.

4. How does love "rejoice in the truth?"

God's truth is revealed less in opinions and more in how we interact with one another, even in our disagreements. God's truth is relational and is revealed not in like-mindedness or "party zeal" but in our learning to love one another. Love is truth! The original word for "truth" means to uncover or reveal. Love reveals God.

5. What is the relationship between love and holiness of heart and life?

The heart of true Christianity is nothing other than love coming to us on its way to someone else. This is God's design (or method) for the church —not to indoctrinate or create systems to separate "us" against "them," or what Wesley calls "pharisaic holiness," where the focus is on outward cleanliness and staying pure. Almost every time Wesley defines holiness, he does so with these fruits or virtues of love—patience, kindness, temperance, and the like. Some theological systems downplay the possibility of inward holiness. These systems focus faith around believing and being outwardly obedient until we reach heaven. Using scripture and experience, Wesley was much more optimistic that our hearts can be transformed into holiness, even in this life.

6. What role does intentionality and discipline play in the fulfilment of this optimistic hope? (A question to span all chapters).

Here is an important word from Wesley (as a paraphrase). "A Methodist is not distinguished by any opinion or scheme of religion that causes us to judge others. All of that is quite wide of the point. A Methodist is one who has the love of God planted in their heart. A Methodist is one who cultivates this love and strives daily to bear the fruits of this love." (From *Character of a Methodist*). Methodism is about "becoming." As incarnate beings, this "becoming" doesn't just happen. It requires intentionality and discipline. As Methodists, we are encouraged to ask: What are we going to do today to become all that God wants for us? What can we do this day to open our hearts to God's transforming love?

CHAPTER FOUR

"Blessed are the Pure in Heart, the Peacemaker, and the Persecuted"

Upon the Lord's Sermon on the Mount – Discourse 3

(A devotional paraphrase)

Sermon 23 in the Standard Sermons of John Wesley

Paraphrase of Wesley sermon

> "Blessed are the pure in heart, for they will see God."
>
> "Blessed are the peacemakers, for they will be called children of God."
>
> "Blessed are those who are persecuted for the sake of righteousness, for theirs is the kingdom of heaven."
>
> "Blessed are you when people revile you and persecute you and utter all kinds of evil against you falsely[a] on my account. Rejoice and be glad, for your reward is great in heaven, for in the same way they persecuted the prophets who were before you."
>
> **Matthew 5:8-12**

Love your neighbor! This directive is the end, or purpose, of the commandments of God. Without this, all we have, all we do, and all we suffer is of no value to God. Where does this love come from? It springs from the love of God. As we have proclaimed over and over again, we are able to love because God first loved us, and God's love always comes to us on its way to someone else.

With that great truth affirmed, what allows this love to flow through us? The answer can be found in "purity of heart." "Blessed are those who are pure in heart." If something is pure, then it is uncontaminated and clean. Purity of heart removes barriers and pollutants that block or pervert God's love. Purity of heart allows God's love to flow freely and abundantly in and through us. The cleansing blood of Jesus purifies our hearts from every unholy affection, opening the way for the patient, gentle love of God to flow in abundance.

We do the church a great disservice when we focus only on abstaining from outward impurities. A big example is when our Lord says, "You have heard it said, 'You shall not commit adultery,'" and many blind leaders of the blind only insist that "men" abstain from the outward act of disobedience. But Jesus says, "Whosoever looks on another with lust has already committed adultery in their heart." God looks upon the heart and works with us at that level. God wants pure hearts *for* us, not just *from* us, not just surface cleanliness on the outside, like "white-washed tombs."

This is serious business, so serious that Jesus challenged us with metaphors intended to shock us into thinking differently. He said, for example, "If your right eye causes you to sin, tear it out … It is better for you to lose one of your parts than for your whole body to be thrown into hell" (Matt 5:29). If any person, or thing, or desire causes you to offend God's will, separate yourself from that contaminant. Do so, first with fasting and prayer, next by being careful to abstain, and then, if needed, ask for counsel from one who is charged with watching over the souls of the congregation.

This sermon from Jesus is all about teaching the religion of the heart. Jesus first shows what Christians are to be and then proceeds to show what we are to do—how inward holiness leads to outward action. So, next, we read, "Blessed are the peacemakers, for they shall be called children of God."

Sometimes, we use the word "peace" to describe separation: you stay on your side; I'll stay on mine, and we'll have peace." Here, peace implies something much more. The Hebrew word "shalom" implies coming together in harmony. The Greek word "Irene" implies active goodwill to all, in all circumstances, in time, and in eternity. Peacemakers are those who detest strife and contention and strive to prevent this "fire of hell from being kindled, or, when it is kindled, from spreading any farther." "They endeavor to calm the stormy spirits, to quiet turbulent passions, to soften the minds of contending parties, and, if possible, reconcile them to each other." That's peacemaking.

As followers of Jesus, peacemakers cannot confine this love only to family or friends, political parties, or those who share like-minded opinions. We are called to "step over all these narrow bounds." The peacemaker rejoices in doing good, to body and spirit, sowing seeds of the kingdom of God anywhere and everywhere. Blessed are the peacemakers, for they shall be called children of God.

One might romanticize this blessing and believe that Jesus, so mild and gentle, so free of selfish design, and so devoted to God, would be loved by all. Our Lord, however, was better acquainted with human nature in its present state. Thus, his next blessing is upon those who are persecuted for righteousness' sake.

Throughout the scriptures, we are reminded not to be

surprised when we see disdain for those who are born of the Spirit (Gal 4:29; 2 Tim 3:12; 1 John 3:13-14; John 15:18). People whose hearts are consumed by power, greed, and the fear that leads them to protect what is known will engage in overt and more subtle forms of persecution. The more the kingdom of God prevails, the more it enrages those determined to keep power and maintain the status quo. The proud must persecute the lowly to build themselves up. The lighthearted must ridicule those who mourn. The religious legalist must put down the openness, tolerance, and inclusiveness required within peacemaking.

As a nation, we have been blessed. God has given us peace. God has caused the pure light of the gospel to shine among us. But what is the response? God looks for righteousness and instead hears a cry— a cry of oppression, of ambition and injustice, of malice and fraud, of covetousness and lust. In this darkness, God will sometimes give us over to our persecutors as a judgment mixed with mercy, a medicine to heal. Seldom, however, will God let the storm rise to the level of imprisonment, torture, or death.

Most often, God's children only endure a lighter persecution—estrangement from family or loss of friends or work. They live Jesus' words: "I did not come to bring peace on earth, but rather division." Persecution will come to all of God's children in some form. It is a badge of discipleship, a seal of our calling. The meek, serious, humble, zealous lovers of God and humanity, who proclaim love for enemies, welcome strangers, seek peace with those in other parties, give mercy to sinners, food to the hungry, and compassion to all may be in good rapport with God and the congregation but in bad rapport with the world.

How might we respond to this persecution? The call is to rejoice and be glad. That may be a hard calling to hear. By this mark, you know to whom you belong and know your reward is great. Therefore, let no persecution turn you from humility and love. Remember the words, "You have heard it said an eye for an eye, and to avenge evil for evil, but I say to you, do not resist evil; turn the other cheek; go the extra mile; do good to those who hate you; return good for evil; pray for those who persecute you." Whether they repent or not, you have proved yourself a child of God by kindness and mercy.

Consider all the beatitudes from these last few weeks and behold the religion of Jesus Christ in its purest form. This is the spirit of true religion, the essence of it. Oh, that we may all be doers of this word and not hearers only. Oh, that we all may give witness to the ways of God, which are definitely not our ways. Let this good word get into your soul so you might go through life with a vision of what God wants for all creation.

Amen.

Mountaintop Blessings

Matthew 5:1-12 (with a focus on 8-12)

If you've not already, you should someday travel to the top of Pinnacle Mountain just outside Little Rock, Arkansas. This mountain is dear to me. I grew up being able to walk out my front door and see this mountain. To share one memory, football season at Joe T. Robinson High School began with the coach taking us to the foot of this mountain and giving us twenty minutes to make it to the top. That was not fun, especially if you had gotten out of shape through the summer. Other than that, I have many fond memories of climbing Pinnacle. From the top of this mountain, I can see my home. I can see the lake, fed by the river, providing water to many. I can see important places in my life and how they connect. It is good to stand on top of a mountain and see things from a higher perspective.

The words of the Beatitudes begin what we call the Sermon on the Mount. At one level, this title simply speaks of where Jesus delivered his message: *from* the mountain. On another level, this sermon is *about* the mountain. Throughout scripture, the mountain represents being closer to God. From the mountaintop, our imaginations are awakened, and we can envision our lives as a part of God's big kin-dom, God's family, God's blessed and beloved community.

From this mountaintop, we see the better way. Instead of trying to build ourselves up, we discover the joy of caring for others and building them up. Instead of focusing on gaining all we can in possessions and power, we see we are poor in spirit from this mountain. We are all in poverty, every one of us. We don't have the resources within ourselves to give greater meaning to life or to connect our hearts to eternity. We learn to receive this blessing as a gift. Those are just some of the blessings we have studied.

Now, we once again take our place on the mountain with Jesus and discover more about how to love others. Love is at the heart of all these beatitudes. They can all be summed up with one word: love. According to Jesus, love is the end, or purpose, of all blessings from God.

And so, we ask, "What allows this love to flow through us?" If it is true that God's love comes to us on its way to others, how can we cultivate this movement? How do we keep this flow of love from being blocked?

The answer is found in the phrase "purity of heart." "Blessed are the pure in heart, for they shall see God." Let's think about purity for a moment. I Googled the words "purity" and "faith," and the first things that popped up were articles about sexuality and advice mainly to youth. Purity, as one article said, means to "pace your passion, to resist feeding your fantasies, to acknowledge the presence of God on every date." It's not bad advice, but it is too easy for us to compartmentalize purity into this one dimension of life. We don't get off the hook that easily.

Jesus says, "Blessed are the pure in HEART." Heart is a metaphor for what is at the center of your life, at the core. The call here is to keep our hearts pure of all pollutants that might block or contaminate God's love: arrogance, greed, anger, envy, and lust. When our hearts are pure, the way is cleared for us to see God and see God's hand over us for good, guiding us into the heights and depths of God's love. "Blessed are the pure in heart, for they shall see God." We can think of what we are doing here as we worship, pray, and receive God's word as a filter that removes contaminants that cloud the way to God. Here, we are being cleansed from the inside out so we can see God.

Next, we read, "Blessed are the peacemakers, for they shall be called children of God." In our world, peace is often used to describe separation: you stay on your side, I'll stay on mine, and we'll have peace. That's not what Jesus has in mind as he gives us this mountaintop perspective. The word he uses implies coming together in harmony. It implies active goodwill to others. That's what children of God do—and not only to family and friends or those in our own political party. As John Wesley says, we must "step over all these narrow bounds." Peacemakers "endeavor to calm the stormy spirits, to quiet turbulent passions, to soften the minds of contending parties, and, if possible, reconcile them to each other." That's peacemaking—and peacemaking is different from peacekeeping, where we often stay silent and hold feelings to avoid tensions. We are called to be peacemakers.

And then we come to the last of these eight beatitudes: "Blessed are those who are persecuted for righteousness' sake, for theirs is the kingdom of heaven." This beatitude is a hard statement to hear. In a sense, I believe Jesus is leading us down the mountain at this point and into the reality of the world. Down here, we must confront the lies that are told every day. We hear them all the time. These lies are the opposite of the beatitudes given to us on the mountain. Blessed are those who have it all together. Blessed are those who focus their lives around power and wealth. Blessed are those who protect the status quo. Blessed are those who divide and conquer. Blessed are those who spend their energy building walls around their hearts. We could go on and on. We know the lies. We may even still hold some of them dear to our hearts. Those who hold on to the lies will not like it when they are challenged with a higher way. Persecution will come—perhaps in the form of ridicule or perhaps in the form of extreme hatred. And yet, we are called to the witness of these beatitudes because, as we share these blessings, transformation will come as well. Our witness amid the lies will lead others to open their hearts to the love of God. That's the greatest blessing.

As you travel, I suspect many of you will find yourselves on a peak where you can see your home from a higher perspective. In fact, I encourage you to do so—if not physically, then in your imagination—and from that place, remember the words of Jesus and the higher vision that he gives. It is the way of true blessings.

Amen.

Reflections for Devotion and Discipling

1. According to Wesley, love is the reason, the way, and the goal. It is the destination and the journey. How can we keep our spiritual eyes, ears, heart, soul, and body focused only on living more fully in the love of God?

As we have seen repeatedly, it all comes down to love. Without love, all we have, do, or suffer is of no value. A key question is, Where does this love come from? The answer leads to a primary theological principle for Methodists, built on many scripture passages, with 1 John 4:19 being used frequently: "We love because God first loved us." Or, to put it another way, "God's love always comes to us on its way to someone else." For us, faith is about opening our hearts to this love, allowing it to transform us, and then taking the risk to live this love in the world.

2. What does it mean to be pure in heart, and why is purity of heart important to our spirituality?

"Purity of heart" allows this love to flow through us. From this perspective, purity is much more than abstaining from outward impurities. It is a matter of opening our hearts to God's work. It is about "inward holiness" that leads to "outward action" (another major tenant of Wesleyan theology, as summarized in the reflection from the last chapter and will be again in future chapters).

3. What does it mean to be peacemakers, and how does this differ from peacekeeping?

After revealing what we are called to be, Jesus shows us what we are to do. The next blessing is to be "peacemakers." This phrase also has depth of meaning. Review its meaning and reflect upon how this calling is different from peacekeeping.

4. The final blessing here has to do with persecution. Why does persecution come to the faithful? What is our response?

Persecution will come to all of God's children in some form. The world will show animosity and hatred against dispositions like meekness, humility, love of enemies, welcoming strangers, seeking peace with those in other political parties, and giving mercy to sinners. Why is this? What is our response, and where do we get the strength?

5. Why are these blessings called "beatitudes?" In summary, how are they different from what the world calls "blessed"?

The word "beatitude" comes from a Latin word describing the condition or "attitude" of being blessed or favored. These eight sayings describe attitudes or ways of living that connect us to the blessings or favor of God. We know the lies that are the opposite of the blessings given here: blessed are those who have it all together; blessed are those who focus their lives around power and wealth; blessed are those who protect the status quo; blessed are those who divide and conquer. We could go on and on. These eight blessings reveal that the ways of God are not the ways of the world. These eight blessings summarize the spirit of "true religion." Wesley then calls us to be "doers of the word and not hearers only" (James 1:22).

CHAPTER FIVE

"Salt and Light"
Upon the Lord's Sermon on the Mount – Discourse 4
(A devotional paraphrase)

Sermon 24 in the Standard Sermons of John Wesley

Paraphrase of Wesley sermon

> *"You are the salt of the earth, but if salt has lost its taste, how can its saltiness be restored? It is no longer good for anything but is thrown out and trampled under foot."*
>
> *"You are the light of the world. A city built on a hill cannot be hid. People do not light a lamp and put it under the bushel basket; rather, they put it on the lampstand, and it gives light to all in the house In the same way, let your light shine before others, so that they may see your good works and give glory to your Father in heaven."*
>
> **Matthew 5:13-16**

The beauty of holiness is apparent to all who have spiritual eyes opened by God. The light that shines from a meek, humble, gentle, patient, loving spirit brightens the life of anyone capable of discerning spiritual good and evil to any degree. This transforming light is beautiful in those moments it is seen. But then we are moved to ask, Why is this light dimmed by so many other things? Why must this pure blessing of religion be encumbered with so many outward rituals and practices?

Some church leaders throughout history have advised that we "cease from all outward action" and "wholly withdraw from the world," with no concern for outward religion but to work all virtues solely from within. Some say this is the most excellent way. I say this is a delusion! It can even be considered a device of Satan, taking some aspect of truth and perverting it. It is true that "retreat" is necessary for spiritual well-being every day. We all need time to converse with God privately and rest the body and spirit. However, allowing "retreat" to become the end rather than the means is to destroy, not advance, true holiness.

Our Lord calls us all to "active religion," where we are directly involved in the world. Jesus says clearly, "You are the salt of the earth" and "You are the light of the world." With these direct statements, it is made clear that Christianity is a "social religion," and "to turn it into a solitary religion is indeed to destroy it." Our faith is cultivated by worshiping, conversing, and serving with others. To be Christian is to grow in humility, patience, and gentleness. These virtues have no place outside interaction with others. In short, our calling in this world is to learn how to love one another and engage in peacemaking, as we have seen. This cannot happen except by intentionally joining together with others.

Some advocate that we only have conversations with those deemed "good" or "holy of heart." Yes, some scriptures advise Christians to avoid "keeping company" with fornicators, idolaters, "railers" (or party zealots), drunkards, extortioners, and the like (1 Cor 5:9). There are other scriptures, however, from the same author, that advise us not to count those who do such things as enemies but to admonish them as a sibling (2 Thes 3:15). There is tension in these pieces of advice, and we must weigh them in the light of key scriptures and evaluate them in the light of the circumstances in which we find ourselves. This discernment is the key to spiritual wisdom.

A place to start is in the words of our Lord found in this portion of the Sermon on the Mount. Here, we see that we cannot be Christian by breaking off all commerce and conversation with the world. Interaction is essential to grow and reveal the temperaments required for living in God's kingdom. Relationship with others, especially those who are different from us, is the only way to exercise "poverty of spirit, mourning, meekness, peacemaking, and every other disposition that marks the genuine religion of Jesus Christ." How could we ever practice turning the other cheek, resisting evil, or loving enemies apart from these virtues?

So, Jesus says, "You are the salt of the earth." Your very nature is to season whatever is around you. You are called to spread the way of Christ to whatever is touched, to be diffused within the community. This is one reason for mingling with others. If the salt has lost its ability to flavor and purify, what purpose does it have? It is good for nothing. If your love has grown flat, if you have become careless with your own soul and useless to the souls of others, how shall you recover? Where is your hope? Only in the One who can transform! You are called to season the world around you with the love of Christ.

Next, know this. No one with this life-giving faith can

hide or keep it to themselves. "You are the light of the world," says Jesus. The love that comes to us through Christ is meant to shine through us as meekness and mercy, purity of heart, and peacemaking. To conceal these blessings or hold them in private is not the way of Christ. Light is meant to shine.

Some object by saying that all outward rituals and service are distractions and pollution to purity of heart. Outward service and corporate practices can indeed cause harm, especially if we mistake the means for the end or believe that true religion is rooted in the outward works of worship, prayer, and service. True religion is not rooted in anything external to the heart. It is rooted in the inmost soul. But if this root is truly planted in the heart, it will put forth branches. It will bear fruit through acts that partake of the same nature as the root. God is pleased with all outward service that flows from the heart and illuminates the love to which we are called.

As the scripture says, we are to present ourselves as a living sacrifice, holy and acceptable to God (Rom 12:1). This is followed by clear exhortations for how we are to practice this faith: by loving one another with mutual affection, by outdoing one another in showing honor, by contributing to the needs of the saints and practicing hospitality to strangers, to name a few (see Rom 12:9-13). In spirit and truth, we are called to make our daily outward work a living sacrifice to God. In everything we do—and buy, sell, eat, and drink—we are to ask, "Does this glorify God?" And yes, if outward practices—even worship and prayer—become the end rather than the means, we are in trouble, and the light we are called to shine is dimmed. It is possible to put away this abuse and keep the blessings.

Therefore, let your light shine—illuminating your humility of heart, your gentleness, your meekness, your sincere concern for the things of eternity, your fervent love for God, and your tender goodwill for all people. Let your light shine so others can see your good works and give glory, not to you, but to God. Let the light in your heart shine through all works of piety and mercy. To enlarge your ability, renounce all "superfluities." Cut off all unnecessary expenses in food, furniture, and apparel. Be good stewards of every gift of God. Cut off all unnecessary expenses of time and needless activities. Do good; suffer evil; abound in the works of the Lord; and know that your labor is not in vain (1 Cor 15:58).

You are the salt of the earth. You are the light of the world.

Amen.

Salt and Light

Matthew 5:13-16

Let me offer a grammar lesson. Exciting, right? Now, before you check out, let me say that this particular grammar lesson might transform your life. Jesus starts the Sermon on the Mount by speaking in the third-person narrative. He says, "Blessed are *they*." Blessed are *those who*. It's not first person (I) or second person (you), but the third-person voice, (they). For the past few weeks, we have explored the Beatitudes, where Jesus gives general, universal blessings that reveal the ways of God: "Blessed are the meek, for *they* shall inherit the earth." "Blessed are the merciful, for *they* will receive mercy." "Blessed are the peacemakers, for *they* will be called children of God." Then, in verse eleven of Matthew's fifth chapter, Jesus shifts. He shifts from the third person to the second person. He turns to his disciples and says, "Blessed are *you*." At this point, these beatitudes are not just general words. Jesus says they apply directly to *you*: *You* are called to be meek and merciful. *You* are called to hunger and thirst for righteousness. *You* are to be a peacemaker.

In these verses, right after the Beatitudes, Jesus continues his teaching and speaks directly to the disciples. He says, "You are the salt of the earth" and "You are the light of the world."

Let's think about salt for a moment. In that day, salt was very valuable. People were actually paid with salt. In fact, our word "salary" comes from the Latin *saltirum*, which means "salt money." Salt was (and is) used as a preservative and a healing agent. It was (and is) essential for life. It was (and is) an important flavoring, adding zest to food. With the metaphor of salt, Jesus is saying, You are valuable, precious, special; without you, the world would lose some of its flavor, some of its life. Just think about what happens when the love of God is sprinkled through us in places like your neighborhood or community. Something great happens. Other people receive a taste of life. Their lives are enriched. "You are the salt of the earth." Don't underestimate yourself. You are that important.

Next, Jesus says, "You are the light of the world." Light, like salt, is important only in what it enables to happen. In other words, we do not stare at a light bulb, but we enjoy what the light bulb enables us to see. We flip on the switch, and darkness is transformed, perspective is given, and fear is released. "This is what you are able to do," says Jesus. You are able to help others see God and know that they are not alone. Therefore, "Let your light shine," not as a spotlight on you but as a light that reveals the love of God—shining with patience and kindness, forgiveness and grace. "You are the light of the world."

And now, one more important language lesson. Jesus is speaking in the indicative, not the imperative. The indicative is a statement of how things are or how they are perceived. An imperative is a command or challenge. Jesus does not say you *should be* the salt of the earth or that you *should be* the light of the world. He is saying that this is who you are. This is how God sees you. You *are* the salt of the earth. You *are* the light of the world. It makes all the difference whether we conceive of being a Christian as something we *ought to be* or something we *are*.

We can compare two different parenting styles. Imagine one parent going to a child and saying, "You need to go make something out of yourself; you need to become somebody." This parent may think they are motivating, but they are motivating with fear, the fear of being seen as worthless unless one proves themselves somehow. Now, compare that to a parent who starts by telling the child how much they are loved, how wonderful they are, how much the parent believes in them, and how much the parent foresees great things for them because of the potential already given them. This is motivating in a different way. This child is able to grow from deep roots of love and possibility rather than from fear.[8]

In this lesson, Jesus does not say, You *can* be my children; you *can* be the salt of the earth if only you do this or believe that. Jesus doesn't say, You *should be* like light. He doesn't say, Go make something out of yourself. Instead, he says—and God through him says—You are my child. You are special. You are important. You are loved. The whole world will benefit from the flavor, perspective, and nourishment you can give. Now, go live as salt. Now, go let your light shine.

Amen.

Reflections for Devotion and Discipling

1. What is the connection between God's work within the heart and our work within the world?

   Some promote withdrawal from the world to keep ourselves pure. Wesley calls this a delusion, even a device of Satan. God does not call us to "retreat" but to "advance" the ways of God. We are called to "active faith" and are willing to interact with those different from us. To be Christian is to grow in humility, patience, gentleness, and peacemaking. We cannot grow in these virtues outside of interaction with others. Wesley wants us to understand the connection between God's work within the heart and our work within the world. True religion is not rooted in anything "external to the heart." It is not about outward practices or obedience. True religion is God's love planted in the heart. And to continue the analogy, plants are meant to "put forth branches" and "bear fruit."

2. How does the metaphor of salt and light speak to how we are to live in the world?

   Like salt, we are called to season the world around us and be diffused within the community. We are valuable. We are able to preserve, enhance, and add joy to life. Like light, we can illuminate God and help others to see love.

3. What practical advice are we given to be salt and light in the world?

To use Wesley's word, to fulfill this calling, we must renounce all "superfluities." We are invited to cut off all unnecessary expenses in food, furniture, apparel, time, and needless activities. The challenge is to be good stewards of every gift of God and consider all we do with the question, "Does this glorify God?"

4. What is the significance of the shift between the third-person "they" to the second-person "you"?

Jesus moves from the general to the personal. He also speaks in an indicative mood, not the imperative. Jesus does not say you should be the salt of the earth or the light of the world. He is saying that this is who you are. This is how God sees you. This pattern is repeated throughout the scriptures. Paul says, "You are the body of Christ." Peter says, "You are a royal priesthood." How does this change our motivation to grow and become all we can be? What difference does it make when someone believes in us and sees the possibilities within us? We often call people to believe in God. We can also affirm that God believes in us.

CHAPTER SIX

"The Fulfillment of the Law"

Upon the Lord's Sermon on the Mount - Discourse 5

(A devotional paraphrase)

Sermon 25 in the Standard Sermons of John Wesley

Paraphrase of Wesley sermon

> "Do not think that I have come to abolish the Law or the Prophets; I have come not to abolish but to fulfill. For truly I tell you, until heaven and earth pass away, not one letter, not one stroke of a letter, will pass from the law until all is accomplished. Therefore, whoever breaks one of the least of these commandments and teaches others to do the same will be called least in the kingdom of heaven, but whoever does them and teaches them will be called great in the kingdom of heaven. For I tell you, unless your righteousness exceeds that of the scribes and Pharisees, you will never enter the kingdom of heaven."
>
> **Matthew 5:17-20**

Some suppose that Jesus was a mere "teacher of novelties," one trying to introduce a "new religion." This is understandable from any who knew nothing but "outward religion," nothing but the "form of godliness." Or it is understandable from those who hoped he would abolish the "old religion" and perhaps bring an easier way to heaven. But our Lord refutes both. He says, "Do not think that I have come to destroy the Law or the Prophets; I have come, not to destroy, but to fulfill."

What "law" is referred to here? It is not the ritual laws containing countless injunctions and ordinances related to the old sacrifices and services of the temple. Jesus, like the prophets before him, denounced these laws. And when many early Christians, including apostles, wanted to insist that Gentiles observe these laws, Paul won the day by arguing that this was "a yoke upon the necks of disciples that even our forbearers could not bear." So, in this sermon, Jesus speaks of another law. He speaks of God's moral law, the eternal rule of God as affirmed by the prophets, the law that is meant to be written not on tablets of stone but upon the heart. The purpose of all the ritual and relational ordinances, not unlike today, was to restrain evil among disobedient and "stiff-necked people." Earthly laws are temporal and conditional. God's moral law is eternal.

Jesus came to "fulfill" this law. The word "fulfill" refers to more than his personal accomplishment. Jesus also makes this law "fully" visible and reveals its importance for living in relationship with God. This law has been at the core of our relationship with God from the beginning. It is at the heart of the religion proclaimed in the law and by the prophets. It is not a "new religion."

Therefore, there is no contradiction between the law and the gospel, as some suppose. The law doesn't pass away in order for the gospel to be established. They are in perfect harmony with one another. At the heart of both is the love of God and love of neighbor. This law is true holiness, which we have consistently characterized by the virtues of love: patience, gentleness, humility, and temperance. As Jesus says, this love is the summary of the law and the promise of the gospel.

A key question for us is, how can we possibly fulfill this high and holy calling? As we answer this question, we remember we are indeed "poor in spirit," lacking the resources to do so. But then we see the promise of God's heart-transforming love. With God, we can grow into the fullness of this calling through faith in Christ Jesus our Lord.

Jesus says, "Whoever breaks one of the least of these commandments, and teaches others to do the same, will be called least in the kingdom of heaven." The word "break" assumes more than a trespass or violation. It is a willful act. It is an attempt to "dissolve" or "untie." The phrase "least of these commandments" points to the little things we assume do no harm, which we easily justify in our minds or excuse because of our weakness. The standards of God will not be lowered for our convenience. There is no allowance for our "one darling lust." God wants more for us.

The phrase "or teach others to do the same" is worthy of our attention. We teach with words but primarily by example. An open drunkard is a teacher of drunkenness. A Sabbath-breaker is constantly teaching others to profane the Lord's calling on our lives. Those ordained to lead congregations need to be especially vigilant if they are to avoid being instruments of darkness and dragging others into the pit by giving witness to a lust for power, by teaching cheap grace, or by overthrowing the deep moral law of God to promote conventions that serve to build up their vision or bless the status quo. As Jesus says, "To those who are given much, of much is required" (Luke 12:48).

Next, we hear that these "shall be called least in the kingdom." In other words, they will have little in God's kingdom on earth as it is in heaven. Remember that the kingdom of God is love, peace, and joy in the Holy Spirit. That's what we forsake by neglecting the law.

It is impossible to have too high esteem for the truth that we are saved by grace, not works, lest no one should boast. But, at the same time, we must declare that there is no faith that does not engage in works of love (Gal 5:6). When we say "believe," we do not mean that we shall step into heaven without holiness, without transformation of heart. There is no salvation without growth in the virtues of the kingdom. Teaching faith without holiness is teaching the way of destruction.

Jesus says that unless our righteousness exceeds that of the Scribes and Pharisees, we shall not enter the kingdom of heaven. Jesus characterizes the righteousness of the Scribes and Pharisees as outward obedience and an external show of goodness. For a good example of this characterization, see the parable of the two men who went to the temple to pray (Luke 18:9-14). The Pharisee prayed to himself that he was not like others and bragged about all his outward acts, like tithing and fasting. In another place, Jesus compares this type of external righteousness with a "white-washed tomb," clean on the outside and full of dead bones on the inside (Matt 23:27-28). True religion is more than the so-called general rules of faith to do no harm, to do good, and attend to the ordinances of God. Such practices are blessed only as they spring from an inward disposition. It may be said that the Pharisees labored to present God with a good life; the Christian seeks to have a holy heart.

But we must not judge these religious leaders too harshly. Don't think it is okay to fall short of their witness. Their goodness is commendable. We all must give an account of our efforts to do no harm, do good, and attend to the ordinances of God. But by grace, we do not stop here. The high and holy calling is to exceed the righteousness of these religious models. Go higher than this. Let your religion be a religion of the heart. Be poor in spirit, made rich by grace alone. Let your soul be filled with gentleness, patience, and love towards all. Exceed the righteousness of the Scribes and Pharisees, and you shall be called great in the kingdom of heaven.

Amen.

Living Above Average

Matthew 5:17-20, 38-48

A few years ago, I used a video for a sermon series entitled "Anything but Average."[9] I want to revisit this theme in a different context. Yes, we can be above average in caring for one another and our world.

Let's discuss the word "average." I read that the average American spends a staggering ten hours a day in screen time—that can be TV, computer, phone, or gaming system. Ten hours! If the average American also sleeps eight hours, that only leaves six hours for other things. Now, for full self-disclosure, if I include the time I work on a computer and the fact that I read mostly from a screen these days, I must admit I fit into this average. Seeing these hard-cold numbers makes me rethink what I want my averages to be. Perhaps related to that average, here's another one: the average American also gives less to the church or charity than a few years ago. One reason is that we are less engaged. We might be too self-absorbed. Our question today is this: can we rise above average?

Jesus dealt with some averages in his day. For example, he said, "You have heard it said, an eye for an eye, and a tooth for a tooth." This was the established law. This was the average expectation, and believe it or not, this average was an improvement over the previous average. Before this law, there were no limits on retaliation and revenge. People might take a life for an eye or burn a village for a knocked-out tooth. So, laws like this one marked the beginning of something much more civilized. These laws brought about a much more equitable average.

But then Jesus came along and challenged his disciples to be above average: "You have heard it said, 'an eye for an eye, a tooth for a tooth, but I say to you, do not resist evildoers or repay evil for evil.'" Instead, respond in a life-giving way that honors the power of forgiveness, mercy, and love. Be above average.

Jesus gives several examples which have made their way into our common vocabulary. I'll show you. Finish this sentence: "Turn the other _____." We know it. Jesus says, "If someone slaps you on your right cheek, turn the other to them as well." The key to this verse is the image of the "right cheek." Most people are right-handed. If a right-handed person punches you with their right hand, they will hit your left cheek. In that day, slapping someone with the back of your hand on the right cheek was an insult. It was a way to embarrass and claim power over another. Jesus calls us to a higher standard. If someone insults you or puts you down, don't stoop to their level. Seek what is good for them. That's the principle here.

Now finish this sentence: "Go the extra _____" (mile, yes). Jesus says, "If anyone forces you to go one mile, go also the second mile." In that day, Roman soldiers could demand that others carry their gear for them, but the law said they only had to carry it for one mile (or about one thousand steps). So, people would count out the steps and then drop the gear as soon as possible. Those who were under occupation hated the fact that the Romans could make them do this. So, once again, they had to be shocked when Jesus told them to offer to go the "extra mile."

The "extra mile" is a metaphor for many things. How might you go the extra mile? One might clean their bedroom and then clean the bathroom as well. One might give money to the food pantry and then show up to help at the Amazing Grace Café and experience the reward of heaven. One might go to a funeral and then go sit with a grieving friend. One might watch the news and then get involved in a cause. When we get up and go the extra mile, we reveal the kind of love God has for all of us. In Christ, God went all the way to the cross to conquer sin and death and open the way of life for us. That's going the extra mile.

Our scripture tells us that Jesus came to fulfill the law or to make God's law fully present. But that's a bit confusing since we know that Jesus was critical of many laws and ordinances written in the books. Like the prophets before him, Jesus denounced many of these laws and considered them a burden. So, what does it mean that he came to fulfill the law? Jesus came to make fully present the higher moral law of God that governs even in heaven. At its core, we are talking here about the great commandments, the summary of all the law, as Jesus says. It is to love God with all your heart, soul, mind, and strength and to love your neighbor as a part of yourself. This law is not just written on tablets, monuments, or in books; it is to be written on our hearts. This law of love inscribed in our hearts raises us above the averages of the world.

Jesus gives an example. He says, as people of God, we don't just love those we know or who are like us. What good is that? That's just average. The way of God is to love even your enemies and seek what is good for them. As members of this blessed and beloved community, we are challenged to live right now by a much higher standard. When we love, we open the doors wide. We make room. We become a part of how God's blessings are poured out in abundance.

So, let's think about "average" again for a moment. The average person, we might say, only hangs out with those who are like them and either ignores or puts down others who are different. The average person promotes revenge. The average person builds walls, including walls around their own hearts. The average person watches life go by rather than living fully and faithfully. In the Sermon on the Mount, we learn that God wants much more for us. You are capable of being blessed beyond worldly measure. Through Christ and with the Holy Spirit, you can excel in goodness, mercy, and love. That's what disciples of Jesus do.

Amen.

Reflections for Devotion and Discipling

1. How does Jesus fulfill the law, and what law does Jesus fulfill?

   Wesley distinguishes between the countless ordinances and rules within the scriptures and the deeper moral law of God that holds all things together in heaven and on earth. Jesus makes this law "fully present."

2. What is the relationship between the law and the gospel? How are we called to something more than "just" faith?

   There are some, especially in Reformation/Protestant circles, that juxtapose law and gospel. The argument is that the gospel, or good news of our redemption through the unmerited love of Christ, has freed us from the law. To be saved, all we need to do is "just believe." Salvation is not based on what we do. In addition, from this perspective, we must avoid any semblance of "salvation by works" or by trying to "establish our own righteousness." Wesley gives us a very different perspective. From a deeper reading of scripture, we see no contradiction between the law and the gospel. Both are rooted in love. Jesus says that love is the summary of the law. We are not freed from this law. By grace, we are called to make this law "fully present" in the world. That is the calling of the body of Christ. The only way to do this is through faith—by actively trusting in God and God's grace and wanting this grace to be at the heart of how we interact with others. Faith is more than "just believing" or affirming doctrines; faith is opening our hearts to God's transforming love. There is no true faith that does not grow out of the love God first gave and that does not desire to work to bring this love into the world.

3. How is "true religion" more than "outward obedience" and keeping the "general rules?"

The Scribes and Pharisees get a bad rap as examples of "outward obedience." They serve as examples of those who follow rules, like our "general rules": do no harm, do good, and attend to the ordinances of God. Jesus has some strong language to describe this understanding of religion. He calls them, for example, "whitewashed tombs." At the same time, he calls us to exceed their righteousness. Their goodness is commendable. We must all give an account of our efforts to do no harm and do good. This sermon is a call to a higher way, a way that leads to true happiness or blessing. We are called to holiness. There are reformation theological perspectives that downplay the possibility of inward transformation. The claim is that we cannot overcome the corruption of sin. Therefore, it is said that faith involves being outwardly obedient and outwardly pure until we make it to heaven. Wesley draws upon this sermon from Jesus to proclaim the possibility of inward holiness and a true transformation of heart in this life. We are to seek after this and devote our lives to it.

CHAPTER SEVEN

"The Lord's Prayer"

Upon the Lord's Sermon on the Mount – Discourse 6
(A devotional paraphrase)

Sermon 26 in the Standard Sermons of John Wesley

Paraphrase of Wesley sermon

"Beware of practicing your righteousness before others in order to be seen by them, for then you have no reward from your Father in heaven.

So whenever you give alms, do not sound a trumpet before you, as the hypocrites do in the synagogues and in the streets, so that they may be praised by others. Truly I tell you, they have received their reward. But when you give alms, do not let your left hand know what your right hand is doing, so that your alms may be done in secret, and your Father who sees in secret will reward you.

And whenever you pray, do not be like the hypocrites, for they love to stand and pray in the synagogues and at the street corners, so that they may be seen by others. Truly I tell you, they have received their reward. But whenever you pray, go into your room and shut the door and pray to your Father who is in secret, and your Father who sees in secret will reward you.

When you are praying, do not heap up empty phrases as the gentiles do, for they think that they will be heard because of their many words. Do not be like them, for your Father knows what you need before you ask him.

Pray, then, in this way:

Our Father in heaven, may your name be revered as holy.

May your kingdom come.

May your will be done on earth as it is in heaven.

Give us today our daily bread.

And forgive us our debts, as we also have forgiven our debtors.

And do not bring us to the time of trial, but rescue us from the evil one.

For if you forgive others their trespasses, your heavenly Father will also forgive you, but if you do not forgive others neither will your Father forgive your trespasses."

Matthew 6:1-15

We are called to put feet to our faith, to act upon what we believe. This is how faith comes alive and indeed shines so others may see our good works and give glory not to us but to God. We engage in acts of goodness to glorify or illuminate the goodness of God, not for self-glorification. So, Jesus says, "When you give, do not sound a trumpet before you."

From here, Jesus moves to what we call "works of piety." "When you pray," he says, "do not do as the hypocrites do, for they love to stand and pray … so they may be seen by others." Hypocrisy is the outward show when actions do not align with our hearts or words. When we pray this way, we cut ourselves off from heavenly rewards.

So, Jesus advises us to go into our personal room, shut the door, and pray in secret. It is a metaphor, suggesting that nothing is a barrier between us and God. As we pour out our hearts to God, God is there to lift us up. In this way of praying, there is no need to try to sound holy or speak at length. It is pure superstition and folly to think that God measures our prayers by their length or eloquence.

The purpose of prayer is not to inform God as though God doesn't already know what's going on. The purpose is to discern God's higher desires for us and seek God's continual guidance and grace. Prayer is not what we do to influence God, who is always more ready to give than we are to ask. It is more about putting ourselves in a place to receive the good things God has prepared for us.

After teaching the nature and purpose of prayer, Jesus gives an example. He gives us a model consisting of three parts: the preface, the petitions, and the doxology.

First, the preface: "Our Father which art in heaven." If God is Father, then God is good and loving to God's children—the first and greatest reason for prayer. God wants to bless us. We are God's children, and God is there to help us grow into all we were created to be.

We say OUR Father—not just mine but the Father of the whole universe, of all families, both in heaven and on earth. In God, we are connected together. In God, we learn to love the world as God does.

We then add, "Which art in heaven," reminding us that God is over all and able to see all.

Next is "Hallowed be thy name." God is the Holy One, always beyond our control and never to be defined by our narrow agendas. God's name is "I am who I am" (Ex 3:13-15). God's ways are not our ways (Is 55:8-9). In praying that God, or God's name, be "hallowed" or "glorified," we are praying that God may be known and honored by all in heaven and on earth. We are praying that we might be aligned with God's ways rather than trying to get God to align with ours.

"Thy Kingdom come." This first petition is connected to the preface. We pray for the kingdom of Christ to come. Remember what the Apostle Paul says about the kingdom: God's kingdom is not "meat or drink" but righteousness, love, peace, and joy in the Holy Spirit. God's kingdom yields both holiness and happiness.

"Thy will be done on earth as it is in heaven." This is the consequence of the coming of the kingdom. With these words, we pray that we and all humankind would do the whole will of God in all things willingly, continually, and perfectly. We pray that the righteousness of God—love, peace, and joy—might come through us.

"Give us this day our daily bread." Here, bread is a metaphor for all things needful, whether for our souls or bodies. We ask for what is sufficient for this day. We do not claim a right to these blessings but only to receive God's free mercy.

"And forgive us our trespasses." The Greek word is also used to describe "debts." Sin is pictured as "falling short." We have nothing to give that could align or justify us to God's will. According to the law, if God were to require what was justly due to God, we would be "bound hand and foot, and delivered over to the tormentors," to use an image from the "debtor's prison." Forgiveness and mercy are our only hope.

Indeed, in a spiritual sense, we are bound by the chains of our own sin. These sins "bring us down to the chambers of the grave." This brings us to the word "forgive," which implies unlocking the chains, giving freedom, and "wiping the slate clean." Forgiveness is rooted in the deepest compassion. With forgiveness, the grip of fear and harm is replaced by love. In this love, there is no condemnation. We are set free. We are able to walk with the Spirit as our guide.

And, if we are given this gift, we are to give this same gift to others: "As we forgive those who trespass against us." God forgives, and then we are transformed to forgive others. Until we can forgive others, we do not truly know forgiveness. Therefore, God forgives us "as" we forgive others. If malice, bitterness, or anger remains in our hearts, God cannot fully forgive us. God may indeed show some mercy, but if we can't forgive, we block God from truly cleansing us of all sin. We hold on to it.

"And lead us not into temptation but deliver us from evil." The word "temptation" also means "trial." Here, "temptation" means something other than "solicitation to sin" or a kind of "enticing." It implies being tried, amid harm and heartache, when we find ourselves in circumstances that have produced anger, envy, impatience, lust, and the like. As the Apostle James says, "Blessed is the one who endures temptation. For when we are tried and approved by God, we receive the crown of life," and then James adds that we should never claim that God tempts us or leads us into temptation because God cannot, and does not, tempt to evil (James 1:12-13). Every temptation comes from being "drawn away" by our own sinful desires. Therefore, we pray that God does not allow us to be led into temptation and ask God to give us the strength to endure. That's the more precise meaning here. The prayer is to be delivered from evil. Jesus reminds us that this force called "evil," which may torment us for a time, cannot destroy us, for God is with us and will not fail us in the end.

And now, we turn to the conclusion. It is a doxology, a statement of praise: "For thine is the kingdom" (the sovereign rule over all things, from everlasting to everlasting), "the power" (the ability to transform), "and the glory" (the illumination of all that is truly good, life-giving, and worthy of our praise) "forever" (pointing us to eternity and the truth that nothing in life or in death can separate us from the love of God through Christ Jesus our Lord, the one who teaches us to pray. Then there is the final word, "Amen!" which means, "Let it be so!"

"Pray like this"

1 Thessalonians 5:16-24; Matthew 6:1-15

Because many of us say the Lord's Prayer almost every week in worship, we might assume that this is a formula of set words with only one way to pray it. However, this prayer has several versions, even in the scriptures. The gospels share different versions from the one we normally say together in worship. So, what do we make of these differences? Well, Jesus is not giving us a formula of set words. Jesus is teaching the disciples how to pray. So, from the very beginning, the disciples added their own words and reflections. In other words, they prayed! They did what Jesus had taught them—not just repeat words but pray this way.

In this lesson, the Greek word for prayer is "pro-euchomai." It has two parts. "Pro" means "to advance" or "move toward." A PROfessional is one who is advanced. Then we have "euchomai," which means "desire" or "hope." So, from this Greek word, we learn that prayer is an "advanced desire," an advanced hope beyond our finite hopes. Prayer is moving away from our human desires and into God's desires for us. Prayer is not so much the words we say as it is the opening of our lives to God's advanced desires and hopes for us.

We begin with the words "Our Father." And even in versions where the word "our" is left out, it is still assumed. One consistent element in all versions of this prayer is that it is plural throughout: our, us, we. So perhaps this is the first truth that Jesus is teaching us about prayer. Prayer is always about more than "me" or "my" needs. In prayer, we are invited into something bigger than ourselves. We are invited into community. That is at the heart of God's advanced desire for us.

"Our Father." The word for father here is "Abba," which suggests an intimacy and close relationship. We are all related in the deepest spiritual sense and connected to our Father, Parent, Creator, Provider, Caregiver, Comforter, and Guide. Being in this close relationship with God is at the heart of God's advanced desire for us.

We pray, "Our Father in heaven." So, where is heaven? We tend to think of heaven as far, far away. Heaven is out there or on the other side of death. Jesus, however, preaches something very different. He teaches that the kin-dom of heaven is in our midst. In another place, he says, the kin-dom of heaven is "within us." God is close. And we get to be a part of bringing the virtues of heaven into the world. We pray for God's love to come to us on its way to others.

"Oh God, may your will be done on earth as it is in heaven."

You may notice I have used the term "kin-dom" in addition to "kingdom." As we discussed in an earlier chapter, both are translations. When we translate this term as "kingdom," it carries some particular images of castles, thrones, and subjects that some may see as outdated. By using the word "kin" (family), we are able to emphasize that Jesus is calling us into community, into God's family, and to know that God is with us. We remember that, even as Jesus used the original word "kingdom," he gave it new meaning and offered a new vision of what this relationship might look like.

Next, we have the one petition in the prayer where we ask God to give us something directly: "Give us this day our daily bread." We ask God to give us what we need to do this work of the kin-dom. From another angle, some see this as an affirmation that God gives us—the whole creation—our daily bread. There is enough for all. If some are hungry—members of our spiritual family—then it is because we have perverted God's design and created an inequity that keeps some from being able to have what they need. Once again, we can pray for God's will to be done through us on earth as it is in heaven.

The next dimension to this teaching on prayer revolves around forgiveness. "Forgive us our sins as we forgive others." The word "forgive" is made of two words: "for" and "give." For a new perspective, reverse these words; change "for give" to "give for." Forgiveness is the active giving to others and helping others to receive what God wants for all of us: healing, peace, and joy.

The word "forgive" is connected to the word "sin." Here, "sin" means to "fall short" or "miss the mark." The word is also translated as "debts," falling short of what we owe, or "trespasses" when we stray from where we need to be. We are called to "give for" when others fall short. We meet them where they are. We make up the difference. We work to align the relationship as God does for us. This is at the heart of God's advanced desire for us.

The last dimension of this teaching about God's advanced desire for us revolves around temptation or trials. It is a matter of interpretation as to how the words are translated. A few years ago, Pope Francis approved a change in translation to say, "Do not let us fall into temptation." This eliminates the misguided thought that God might lead us into temptation or trials. God does not do that (see James 1:13-14). My personal favorite is to ask God to bring us through temptation. Temptation and trials do come. God is there to see us through and bring us into God's advanced hopes for us.

I invite you to pray the Lord's Prayer—not simply saying the words but pondering what they mean and how they challenge and transform us into all God wants for us. I hope you will let these words profoundly inspire and guide you. I invite you to make this your prayer.

Amen.

Reflections for Devotion and Discipling

1. What does it mean to say that prayer is a means of grace? Do you (we) give enough attention to these means?

   The idea of means of grace is very important to Methodism. Our denominational name comes from the disciplined attention to these means. Wesley names different means of grace in different lists, but prayer is always there. Prayer is a God-given means or method that leads to the unfolding of God's grace in our lives and our world.

2. What is the purpose of prayer? What does the Greek term for prayer reveal to us?

   Though the means of grace are important to Methodism, "true religion," or true holiness, is always more important. Prayer is more than words or an obligation to fulfill. Prayer is a means that leads us into God's higher desires for us and for the world. Review this understanding in the sermon.

3. Review the "preface" of the Lord's Prayer. How is this a model for us?

   Jesus devotes a significant amount of time to prayer. He gives us a model and reveals important dimensions of prayer that can move us into God's advanced desires for us. The first words are addressed to God as a reminder of who God is.

4. Review the "petitions" of the Lord's Prayer. What do they model for us?

We often think of prayer as asking God to give. From this model, we see that prayer does include petitions. The question is, are we asking for the right things? Are our desires aligned with God's will?

5. Review the "doxology" of the Lord's Prayer. How is this a model for us?

Praise and thanksgiving are an important part of prayer, connecting us to God, helping us see what is worthy of praise, and drawing us away from our own perspectives so we can see reality as part of the kin-dom of God. The last word in this model prayer is "forever." What is important about this word?

CHAPTER EIGHT

"On Fasting"
(and modeling the middle way)

Upon the Lord's Sermon on the Mount – Discourse 7

(A devotional paraphrase)

Sermon 27 in the Standard Sermons of John Wesley

Paraphrase of Wesley sermon

> *"And whenever you fast, do not look somber, like the hypocrites, for they mark their faces to show others that they are fasting. Truly I tell you, they have received their reward. But when you fast, put oil on your head and wash your face, so that your fasting may be seen not by others but by your Father who is in secret, and your Father who sees in secret will reward you."*
>
> **Matthew 6:16-18**

There is an ongoing theological battle where outward religion is pitted against inward religion as if this is an either/or equation. In one extreme corner, we have "Showtime," who believes that righteousness is all about doing the right things—going to church, wearing the T-shirt, praying in public, handing out food, all to show God and everybody else how good we are. "Showtime's" motto is "Just look at how good I am."

And in the other extreme corner, we have "Just Believe."

"Just Believe" says that righteousness is not about works; it is all about faith. All you have to do is believe, as in giving an appropriate affirmation using the right words. Beyond this, do what you want. Don't focus too much on being good, lest you succumb to the temptation of "works-righteousness" or think you can earn your way into God's good graces. It is better not to try beyond basic niceness and outward morality. "Just Believe's" motto might be "Just Believe."

These two extremes are real in the church. Each side beckons others into its camp. In these camps, any kind of bipartisanship is suspect. And yet, it is good to note that the words "partisan" or "party" include the word "part." A party is part of a larger whole. Therefore, in such camps, we shut ourselves off from at least half the blessings God wants for us. God's ways are always bigger than any part. And, by the way, here we are talking about the church, not the state—although there may also be some implications for the state. Only by meeting with those with different perspectives can we learn how to love.

Can we not steer a middle way? That is a question we continue to ask ourselves in these Standard Sermons. Can we not stand up for grace AND holiness together? In this middle ground, we see that grace without holiness is cheap grace. Cheap grace says, "It doesn't matter what we do because God is gracious anyway." We do not advocate for that. On the other hand, holiness without grace is equally unhealthy. Holiness without grace becomes judgmental, legalistic, and self-righteous. When we go to this extreme, we draw hard lines in the sand and divide the world into "us" and "them."

Both extremes bring much harm into the world, even as we think we are building ourselves up. Can we not bring "Showtime" and "Just Believe" together? As Methodists, we proclaim that there is no faith that does not manifest itself in works of love (Gal 5:6). Faith and works go together.[10]

So, what does all this have to do with fasting? This means of grace illustrates this battle more than any other. At one extreme are those who exalt this discipline beyond what the scriptures say and beyond reason, believing fasting is the perfect discipline to prove how loyal and holy we are. At the other extreme, this discipline is simply ignored altogether. Maybe we think about it during Lent and try it for a day after the pastors have insisted, but it is not a regular part of our spiritual walk with God.

First, fasting means to abstain from food. To fast is to intentionally be hungry for a prescribed time. In the scriptures, we see many examples. We see the example of a one-day fast during daylight hours, from morning to evening. We see fasts for extended periods, even forty days. In the church tradition, we see the call to abstain from particular foods for a time or consume smaller portions. This might be recommended for those who, for health reasons, should not engage in a fuller form of fasting.

The witness of scripture abounds. Through the prophet Joel, the Lord calls us to "sanctify a fast" and to "return to the Lord with all our hearts." In doing this, we discover, once again, that God is "gracious and merciful, slow to anger, and abounding in steadfast love" (Joel 2:12-16). We also have the witness of many others, including Jesus. In our passage for this chapter, we are given specific instructions on how to give alms, fast, and pray. We are given the clear command to perform all these duties as means of grace.

One might naturally fast when they are in a state of grief or emotional struggle, but this is not the same as a spiritual fast. One might fast to lose weight or combat overindulgence. This may have benefits. Excess of food or drink can harm the body and the soul and indeed "chain the soul down to earth." But this is still not the primary reason for fasting as a spiritual discipline. The primary reason for fasting is to help us pray and commune with God.

Prayer and fasting go together. Fasting makes prayer about something more than words. With fasting, we involve our whole being. In both a physical and spiritual sense, we open a place in our lives for God to come in and fill us with the blessings God wants for us. God has given us these practices as channels for grace and growth. Through these disciplines, God is often pleased to lift us up and "sometimes to rap us up, as it were, into the third heaven," providing special strength, guidance, and inspiration.

Some still might object, saying we should fast from sin but not from food. They might argue that this outward work makes it about us. I say that it is not an either/or. God asks for both. The scriptures call us to fast physically and spiritually in faith. Fasting can become a sacramental act, a tangible, physical offering that opens the way for God's grace to come. It is an incarnate act for incarnate beings.

The next question is how. First, we must do so with a focus on God, not ourselves. In this passage, Jesus refers to how some covered themselves with dust and ashes to get attention from others. Truly, says Jesus, they have their reward. We do not engage in spiritual disciplines to "establish our own righteousness."

Fasting is a work of repentance and an act of spiritual cleansing. It is a tangible way for us to open a place in our lives for the transforming grace that renews us to the image of God (2 Cor 7:9). To this end, fasting should always be joined to prayer. And to fasting and prayer, add giving and all works of mercy. There is a direct connection here as well, stated so clearly by the prophet Isaiah: "Is not this the fast that I choose; to loose the bonds of injustice ... to let the oppressed go free? Is it not to share your bread with the hungry and bring the homeless into your house? Then, your light shall break forth like the dawn, and your healing shall spring up quickly ... Then you shall call and the Lord will answer, you shall cry for help and he will say, 'Here I am'" (Isa 58:6-9).

That's how we are to fast! The inward blessings of this means of grace lead to outward good works in the world. Through this discipline, we join faith and works together. We bring the blessed parts into a larger whole and become more whole in the process. That is the promise contained in this means of grace.

Amen.

Making Room

Matthew 6:1-6, 16-21

I have helped move my children out of our home, whether to go to college or move to a different city or state for a new job. Such moves mark the beginning of a new relationship and a big change. Imagine the emotions sparked in such moments. In these moments, I have told myself that this is a good thing. I have believed that in my head, but it has not been as easy in my heart. It is hard to let go. Spending my spiritual energy trying to "hold on" or keep things the same and in a place that fits into my comfort zone is so tempting.

Have you ever tried to hold on to something? The scriptures call us to a hard truth. Time marches on. Things change. Life has a way of making room for new acts of beauty, new opportunities for contributing, and new voices to be heard. We are called to honor this movement and even cultivate it. We do so by developing the important spiritual skill of "letting go" and letting ourselves be blessed by what is to come.

This image of letting go is powerful and can help us hear what Jesus is saying to us today in his Sermon on the Mount. In this sermon, Jesus invites us to let go through three important means of grace: giving, prayer, and fasting. These disciplines are the hard, spiritual work to which we are called. Through this work, we let go of our delusions of holding on and securing our own way. We let go of our trust in the treasures of this world. We let go of our need to keep others in a place that makes *us* comfortable. With all three of these disciplines, we let go and then let God in. We make room for God to come in and fill us with the blessings God wants for us. That is hard when the clutter of our lives leaves little room for the blessings of God.

Let's look at these three disciplines. First, giving—and here we are specifically talking about the giving of money. Jesus talked a lot about this, as much as he talked about anything. In our lesson today, Jesus says, "When you give, sound no trumpet before you." In other words, don't make a show of it. Don't use your giving to make yourself look good before others. Don't use your generosity as leverage for that position or prestige you want. Don't seek to control the outcome. Give because you want to connect this world to God's eternal blessings. Give to bring the treasures of heaven into your life and into the world.

Giving is so important, but not because God *wants* our money. God wants us to open a place in our lives for the blessings God wants for us. We miss these blessings when we try to hold on and are consumed by consuming, filling our lives with what we think we want. In giving, we make room for God.

Next is prayer. We focused on this in detail in the last lesson. For a quick review, prayer is also about us making room. The primary word for prayer in the original language means "advanced desires." Prayer is exchanging our little desires for God's desires for us. Prayer is opening ourselves to all God wants for us and the world. Here is one example. In the way of praying that Jesus taught, we work at forgiving so we can be forgiven. In prayer, we let go of our anger, resentment, and judgmentalism to allow God's forgiveness and grace to fill our lives. If we hold on to these harmful dispositions in our lives, there is simply not much room left for God to come in.

The next means of grace, or spiritual discipline, Jesus mentions is "fasting." Fasting is the one we tend to conveniently ignore. Why would we intentionally make ourselves hungry? And that's what fasting is: intentional hunger. It can be done in many ways. The most common way in the Bible is a daylong fast from sunrise to sunset. There are multiple-day fasts and fasts where we give up certain foods for a period of time.

With all these forms of fasting, the principle is the same. Fasting allows us to let go and let God in. However, fasting has a direct physical effect. With fasting, prayer becomes about something more than words. It affects us in the gut. We quickly learn that we depend on others and God for our well-being. Through prayerful hunger, we are led to God and a desire for God's life-giving, nurturing grace. In a real and physical way, we learn that we do not "live by bread alone." That is so important for us to know, not just in our head but also in our gut.

Through these disciplines, we let go of our stuff and make room for God to come in. For an analogy, have you ever gone shopping and got a great deal on something, only to get home and discover there is no more room in the closet, cabinet, or garage? Has that ever happened to you? Does your stuff spill over into other spaces? This is also an analogy for our spiritual lives and the hard, spiritual work to which we are called.

Through giving, prayer, and fasting, we make room. We make room for mercy, and in this Sermon on the Mount, we hear our Savior say, "Blessed are the merciful." We make room to grieve over all the harm done in the world, and we hear our Lord say, "Blessed are those who mourn." We make room for peacemaking by opening our hearts to forgiveness and understanding, and we hear Jesus say, "Blessed are the peacemakers."

We are called to this spiritual work. We are called to intentionally engage in these practices of faith: giving, prayer, and fasting. We don't engage in these disciplines to show God how strong we are but to discover how strong God is. We don't give, pray, and fast to show others how good we are but to know how good God is. Even when we fail or fall in our spiritual work, it is a way to learn and experience even more of God's forgiveness and steadfast love.

Here is the challenge. Let go. Make room. Do so in real and tangible ways. Make prayer more than words. Prayerfully give. Prayerfully fast. I especially want to challenge you to fast because we ignore this discipline the most and because the blessings that come can be so great and rewarding. Start small. Give up a meal. Sacrifice the cookie or the bowl of ice cream. Invite God in. Trust that you will be blessed. The rewards from God, as Jesus says, will come in abundance.

Amen.

Reflections for Devotion and Discipling

1. What is the "middle way," and why is it the way of faithfulness and fruitfulness?

   Extremism is at work in the church. In this sermon, Wesley gives extremism a theological twist that we may not expect. At one extreme, we see a focus on outward religion, obedience to doctrine, and doing the right things. The other extreme is focused on personal religion, where all you have to do is "just believe." It's all about a personal and vertical relationship through Christ. Wesley consistently wanted to "steer a middle way" and see the blessings of both sides on this spectrum. The Wesleyan way is the way of both/and rather than either/or. We navigate this middle way between grace and holiness, knowledge and piety, evangelism and social justice, and even between progressive and traditional views.

   There is nothing mediocre or wishy-washy about this middle way. It takes great spiritual fortitude to hold this life-giving tension. The middle way is the radical way in the sense of what is central, fundamental, and necessary for the kind of life God wants for us: abundant, blessed, and eternal. This is the way of life found in the radical and often unexpected virtues lifted up in this sermon.

2. Wesley uses the "middle way" to explore the means of grace of fasting. What are your initial thoughts and feelings about fasting?

   According to Wesley, many of us fall into one of these extremes when it comes to fasting. Either we are all in or ignore it altogether.

3. How is fasting different from dieting? What spiritual attitudes are needed for fasting?

Review the sermon and explore the aspects of this means of grace. Are you willing to fast or move towards fasting using one of the models given?

4. What is the relationship between fasting, prayer, and works of mercy?

Although Wesley focused on fasting in his sermon, he does connect this means of grace to the others mentioned in the scripture passage.

5. How is giving a means of grace? How would you describe the spiritual purpose of giving?

Wesley will fully deal with this means of grace in the next sermon. Here, we try to make the point that giving is important, not because God wants something from us, but because God wants blessings for us. How does disciplined giving open a spiritual place in our lives for God to come in?

6. How do the disciplines of fasting, prayer, and giving teach us the importance of letting go? Why is letting go important to our spiritual well-being? What steps might you take to let go and make room?

These disciplines help us overcome the delusion of holding on and securing our own way. As we practice letting go, we also allow God to come in.

CHAPTER NINE

"Treasures in Heaven"

Upon the Lord's Sermon on the Mount – Discourse 8
(A devotional paraphrase)

Sermon 28 in the Standard Sermons of John Wesley

Paraphrase of Wesley sermon

"Do not store up for yourselves treasures on earth, where moth and rust consume and where thieves break in and steal, but store up for yourselves treasures in heaven, where neither moth nor rust consumes and where thieves do not break in and steal. For where your treasure is, there your heart will be also.

"The eye is the lamp of the body. So if your eye is healthy, your whole body will be full of light, but if your eye is unhealthy, your whole body will be full of darkness. If, then, the light in you is darkness, how great is the darkness!

Matthew 6:19-23

Intentions matter! We hope our labor and relationships will be a "proper offering to God." For practical examples, if we pursue our business for our own honor and riches, we are no longer serving God. We will no longer be connected to the blessings of God any more than if we gave an offering only to be seen by others. We cannot separate sacred and secular activity so easily, for God is at work in all and through all. Our Lord calls us to worship and work with the "same piety of heart."

In our lesson today, Jesus uses the metaphor of the eye to explain this truth. It is about focus. If our spiritual eyes focus on what is good, true, and worthy of praise, we will be guided into the light. If, on the other hand, the eye is focused on evil, even if we think of it as good, then we will be consumed by darkness. In this metaphor, the eye is the intention. What the eye is to the body, intention is to the soul. As the eye guides the body's motions, intentions guide the soul. Clouds will rise if our spiritual eyes turn from a single focus on God. Doubts and fears will come. We will find ourselves "tossed to and fro," blown about by the winds of desires. We will be unfocused and easily lost (Eph 4:14).

The light of Christ shining in us illuminates the holiness to which we are called. In this light, we see that true holiness is not found in judgment, division, or any semblance of the self-righteousness we sometimes associate with religion. Christ's light illuminates the way of love. This love is revealed in humility, gentleness, patience, and all the fruits that glorify God. As we walk in this light, we are transformed into the image of Christ from one degree of glory to another by the Spirit of the Lord (2 Cor 3:18).

Next, this light is characterized by happiness. Holiness and happiness go together. This light brings joy, peace, assurance, and comfort. As we walk in the light of God, we are able to rejoice, pray without ceasing, and give thanks in all things (Phil 4:4-7). In sum, this light guides us into holy happiness.

But we are so prone to stray. We give into desires and temperaments that promise so much but only yield what is "unprofitable, corrupt, and grievous to the Holy Spirit." As we move into darkness, the shadows only bring discontent, division, and even destruction. Thus, our Savior gives straightforward advice: "Do not store for yourself treasures on earth, where moth and rust consume and where thieves break in and steal but store up for yourselves treasures in heaven." We may compare ourselves, as good Christians, with the natives in America. My observation is that Native Americans are, on the whole, equally temperate, sober, humble, and chaste as the natives of England, commonly called Christians. However, when it comes to this word from the Lord, we must give preeminence to the so-called "heathens." In my observance, they model contentment with plain food and clothing and are far less interested in storing up treasures on earth. They more readily live the prayer, "Give us this day our daily bread." Too often, even seemingly good Christians pay little attention to this concept. Certainly, in the pursuit of increased worldly goods and pleasures, many avoid stealing or defrauding others and engage this goal in a principled manner. However, the focus is still on how to properly build earthly treasures. It is amazing how we can easily deceive ourselves as we judge others.

To be clear, we are not forbidden to provide for ourselves and our families. We are not forbidden what is needed to carry out our worldly business. But we can so easily go beyond this focus and store up more than is necessary to fulfill these noble purposes. To do this is to openly deny our faith in the Lord who provides.

You may be highly esteemed by people and, at the same

time, be an "abomination to the Lord." How long shall your souls cleave to the dust? When will you awaken and be persuaded to choose the better treasure? When will you seek only to lay up treasures in heaven? Doing otherwise is to turn your heart over to what is finite, temporal, and lacking in power to give any true and lasting meaning. It is to side with death itself.

In this regard, our Lord tells us that it is harder for a camel to go through the eye of a needle than for a rich person to enter the kingdom of God. It is hard for the rich not to think of themselves as better than the poor. It is hard for us not to seek happiness in riches or become dependent and protective of them. The story of the rich young ruler is illuminating. He sincerely wanted to know what he needed to be saved. Jesus tells him to sell all and follow him. He could not do it. Wealth is not evil in itself, but the desire for it leads us down the darker path (1 Tim 6:10). How shall we escape this fate? As Jesus says, with us, it is impossible, but with God, all things are possible (Matt 19:26).

With spiritual wisdom, let us cry aloud. Do you put your trust in uncertain riches? Will they protect us from any sickness, disease, or pain? Do such realities visit the poor only? No. And there is greater trouble at hand than all of these. Death will come. Our riches cannot "re-animate this breathless clay." We cannot take any of it with us.

Likewise, do not trust in riches for happiness. To do so is the greatest folly under the sun. An abundance of things stored up on earth only brings added stress and misery. Put your trust in the living God, and you shall be safe under the shadow of the Almighty. God's faithfulness shall be your shield. And even when this house of earth is ready to turn back to dust, God's word remains: "O death, where is thy sting? O grave, where is thy victory? Thanks be to God who gives victory through Christ Jesus our Lord" (1 Cor 15:53-56).

"Do not store for yourself treasures on earth." This commandment is as sure as "Do not steal." If we do not use our resources to do good for others, we use them to hurt ourselves—nourishing ill tempers, indulging foolish passions, and supporting vanity. Following these pursuits is like keeping money from the poor to buy poison for ourselves.

Therefore, "Store for yourself treasures in heaven, where neither moth nor rust can corrupt and where thieves do not break in and steal." The wise steward seeks to be rich in good works, giving freely to support the work of the Lord to feed the hungry, welcome the stranger, defend the oppressed, and heal the sick.

By your endeavors to share the blessings of God's love, may you also be able to await in joy for that great hour when the King of Kings shall say, "I was hungry and you gave me food. I was thirsty and you gave me something to drink. Come now, receive the kingdom prepared for you from the foundation of the world" (Matt 25:34-40).

Amen.

Treasures and Stuff

Matthew 6:19-23

I have a self-imposed rule always to have room for our cars in the garage. When I lived in a dorm or apartment, I had to run to the car in the rain or scrape off the frost or ice in the winter. Ironically, this space, created to protect our vehicles, has become, in many instances, a storage room for all our other stuff. I am proud to say that we can get two cars in our garage, but this has sometimes required some creativity and calculation. It can be a challenge to see how high the boxes can be stacked around the outer walls.

Where do you stack your extra stuff? Notice, I just assumed you have extra stuff that you think you might need someday or that will bring you a sense of happiness someday. Where is all that stuff that you trip over today because of the blessings it might give tomorrow?

Jesus speaks to this tendency very directly. He says, "Do not store up your treasures here on earth." It is easy to make excuses: This stuff is not my treasure. I'm not attached to this stuff. Then why do I keep adding to it? Why is it so hard to let go? Why do we get so invested in letting our stuff consume us and think it will make life more meaningful somehow? We all do it at some level.

Jesus offers us an alternative: "Store for yourself treasures in heaven." These treasures, says Jesus, are not subject to decay, rust, or thieves. John Wesley often made lists of heavenly treasures, almost always including patience, kindness, gentleness, humility, compassion, and bearing one another in love. These are heavenly treasures,

treasures that lead to true happiness. These treasures lead to "holiness of heart and life," to use a phrase that Wesley used over and over again.

For Wesley, these were not just words. He intentionally and methodically put himself in places where God's treasures could grow. Here's one of many examples from his journals about investing in the poor. In his journal in 1753 Wesley says, "I visited as many more as I could. I found some ... half-starved both with cold and hunger, added to weakness and pain. But I found not one of them unemployed, who was able to crawl about the room. So wickedly, devilishly false is that common objection, 'They are poor only because they are idle.' If you saw these things with your own eyes, how could you then lay out money in ornaments and superfluities?"

This is an example of the regular work of Wesley and the people called Methodists in that day. And it is in our blood as well. We believe that faith is manifested in good works, and by good works, we mean actually investing in people's lives with the treasures of heaven. Jesus then says, "Where your treasure is, there your heart will be also." Wherever we invest our time, energy, and money, our hearts will follow.

There is a story that has been circulating in the church from the earliest days. The story comes from when the Church was being persecuted by the Roman Empire. A group of Roman soldiers stormed into a church and demanded all their treasures. "Bring us your treasures," they ordered. A deacon of the church pointed at the widows and orphans being fed, the sick being nursed, and the poor whose needs were being supplied and said, "These are the treasures of the Church."

I continue to be haunted and attracted to the story Jesus tells in Matthew 25. This story reveals why we must pay attention to all this. Jesus tells a story of the king of glory sitting on the throne, with all the nations gathered before him, and separating the sheep from the goats, removing all that is not fit for the kin-dom. (As an aside, perhaps this judgment and this removal of evil takes place in each of us, with the hope that we will then be able to recognize ourselves after this purification happens. Ponder that possibility! Would you, or will you, be able to recognize yourself after Jesus makes you fully ready for heaven?) In this judgment, as told in Matthew, the Savior will turn to the sheep and say, "Come, you that are blessed by my Father, inherit the kingdom prepared for you from the foundation of the world; for I was hungry and you gave me food. I was thirsty and you gave me something to drink; I was a stranger and you welcomed me. Then, they will answer him, "Lord, when did we see you and give you something to eat or drink? When did we see you and welcome you?" And here's the answer: "Truly I tell you, just as you did it to one of the least of these who are members of my family, you did it to me."

The lens through which we see the world makes all the difference—and we are called to stay focused. Jesus uses the eye as a metaphor. If our eyes are out of focus, we need extra help to avoid danger. It is the same with our spiritual eyes. For a telling story, a few years ago, our car insurance agent was involved in an accident. He said, "I've heard it a million times—someone is driving down the road and gets distracted. In my case, it was some papers in the back seat. I looked away for only a second, but when I looked back at the road, I was barreling toward a slow-moving pickup with my cruise control set on seventy and nowhere to go. Several thousands of dollars later," he says, "I learned my lesson." So, Jesus warns us about our spiritual vision. If our vision of God becomes blurred or we look away into the darkness, it may not be long until our lives are in a spiritual wreck.

The vision and calling before us are given. Spend your time, energy, and resources storing up treasures in heaven, storing up relationships of love, storing up acts of kindness and compassion, forgiveness and grace. When we do this, we also discover true happiness. Do you want that? True happiness. And just to warn you one more time, the clutter can get in the way, and when the clutter becomes our focus, our priority, then the light of true happiness and holiness is dimmed. May this word today give enough of a glimpse that you will want to move and grow into the very treasures of God.

Amen.

Reflections for Devotion and Discipling

1. As always, Wesley is interested in how we apply theology, not just what we think about it. How might we engage in our work and relationships in ways that are a "proper offering to God"? How especially can we do this with our money and resources?

   In another sermon, which we will see in another volume, Wesley gives us three time-honored principles for how we use our money: gain all you can, save all you can, and earn all you can. To gain all you can means more than accumulating wealth; it can also be understood in terms of knowledge, relationships, etc. To save is more than keeping in reserve. For Wesley, it is about frugality and living simply. To give is to "lay up treasures in heaven" and to make room for the "immeasurable riches of God's grace." Tying these together, Wesley does not focus on a legalistic standard for giving; rather, he encourages us to see that all life is holy, and with every purchase, expense, and act of giving, we can ask: "Does this glorify God? Am I being a good steward of all that God has given me?"

2. What treasures from heaven are we called to share in the world?

Once again, Wesley makes a connection to holiness. And once again, we see that holiness is not found in judgment or divisiveness, sometimes associated with religion, but in love revealed through humility, gentleness, patience, and the rest. How do we live to share these treasures from heaven? What practices are needed for us to "make room" for this holy work?

3. How do we stray and come to focus more on worldly gain and the pursuit of selfish pleasures? What are the spiritual consequences? What causes us to be attracted to the darkness?

There are temptations in the world that promise so much but only yield what is "unprofitable, corrupt, and grievous to the Holy Spirit." When we lack focus, we find ourselves "tossed to and fro," blown about by desires that do not advance us along the path of life.

4. What thoughts are sparked by Wesley's encounter with Native Americans?

Encountering people from other places or cultures helps us see our common humanity. Seeing their goodness can also help us see our shortcomings and where we might have strayed.

CHAPTER TEN

"Seek First the Kingdom of God"

Upon the Lord's Sermon on the Mount – Discourse 9

(A devotional paraphrase)

Sermon 29 in the Standard Sermons of John Wesley

Paraphrase of Wesley sermon

"No one can serve two masters, for a slave will either hate the one and love the other or be devoted to the one and despise the other. You cannot serve God and wealth.

> *"Therefore I tell you, do not worry about your life, what you will eat or what you will drink, or about your body, what you will wear. Is not life more than food and the body more than clothing? Look at the birds of the air: they neither sow nor reap nor gather into barns, and yet your heavenly Father feeds them. Are you not of more value than they? And which of you by worrying can add a single hour to your span of life? And why do you worry about clothing? Consider the lilies of the field, how they grow; they neither toil nor spin, yet I tell you, even Solomon in all his glory was not clothed like one of these. But if God so clothes the grass of the field, which is alive today and tomorrow is thrown into the oven, will he not much more clothe you—you of little faith?*
>
> *Therefore do not worry, saying, 'What will we eat?' or 'What will we drink?' or 'What will we wear?' For it is the gentiles who seek all these things, and indeed your*

heavenly Father knows that you need all these things. But seek first the kingdom of God and his righteousness, and all these things will be given to you as well.

So do not worry about tomorrow, for tomorrow will bring worries of its own. Today's trouble is enough for today."

Matthew 6:24-34 – "Seek First the Kingdom of God"

The Assyrians conquered Israel, and to create unity in the Assyrian Empire, the policy was to mix people up. Many in Israel were exiled to other lands, and others from around the empire were placed in Israel. Over time, people from other places came to "fear the God of Israel" while also serving the gods they had brought with them (see 1 Kings 17).

Are there not parallels to most modern Christians in this scenario? Many engage in some outward services (going to worship, doing some good deeds, and having a measure of faith) while also serving their own gods (silver and gold, pleasures and praise).

Like the people from around the Assyrian Empire, many Christians believe they are within the faith, but it is doubtful they possess an unwavering commitment to the commandment to have no other gods before the Lord. We are told that we "shall worship the Lord our God and serve only him." Following this same line of thought, Jesus says we "cannot serve two masters." The consequences are clear when we attempt to do so: We will end up loving one and hating the other. We will discover not only that we *should not* serve two masters but we *cannot*.

In origin, "Mammon" was the name of a pagan god who presides over riches. Here, Jesus uses "mammon" for the riches themselves. This term represents all resources used to secure our own ease, honor, and pleasure. What is it to serve mammon? First, it implies trusting in riches for our happiness and well-being. It implies that our first aim is increasing wealth with little reference to things eternal. This focus leads us into an earthly, sensual mind, chained to the things of earth, with the desires and temperaments accompanying this passion. This focus does not open the way to life but only increases anxiety.

What is it to serve God? First, this service requires faith. Faith entails trust in God as our source of strength and guidance and recognizes that God is the One who gives us purpose. This faith leads to love for God and all creation. We desire to reflect God's goodwill through all kindness and compassion. That's what it means to serve God in the most general sense.

If we trust Christ for our help and happiness, we cannot trust in riches. Conversely, if we love the world and conform to its ways, then we are not being renewed by the Spirit of God. Let us heed the words of Jesus, "You shall worship the Lord your God and serve only him." To attempt to serve both God and mammon is to be pulled in competing directions, like fire and water, light and darkness. There is no way to experience the joy of faith in this tension. One might find just enough religion to breed misery.

Serving only God does not mean we should be without care for the concerns of life. Neither does it call for sloth or laziness in business. A Christian abhors sloth and idleness as much as drunkenness or adultery. It is God's will that everyone should labor to eat bread and provide for their own household. This cannot be done without effort, focus, careful planning, and creativity. Such work also contributes to the needs of society and brings goodness into the world. Our Lord condemns anxious concerns of the heart that drain the spirit and cultivate fear, which leads us to the next exhortation.

Jesus continues his discourse by speaking of worry and anxiety, especially around food, drink, and clothing. He asks, "Is not life more than these things?" A little later, he tells us to "seek first the kingdom of God and God's righteousness." As we have seen, God's righteousness is always characterized by love—the love of God and all humankind, flowing from faith in Jesus Christ and producing every right disposition of the heart. This focus opens the way of life. It opens the way to faith, where we can trust that God will provide for our needs and be there to see us through. In this faith, we give ourselves over to God's providential care and eternal grace, and we do so daily. If we live another day, God will provide for that as well.

Some might fantasize about how they will serve when other hindrances are out of the way. Others might say they will serve when they feel more of God's presence. Do not deceive yourself. As Jesus says, one who is faithful with a little will also be faithful with much. It is self-deceptive to think you will be faithful only when you have much. In the parable of the talents, the one who is only given one talent does not invest it, and the consequence is that this one talent is taken away and given to another who did invest what was given to them (Matt 25:14-30). The effects of these delusions can be seeds that grow weeds into generations to come.

Therefore, be faithful today. Don't worry about what tomorrow might bring. The future in this world is not yours. We know the sobering truth. From the beginning of time, all generations have gone away and, in many ways, are forgotten. These generations lived their days and then were shaken off the earth like leaves off a tree. Ashes to ashes, dust to dust! New generations come desiring to find their own way. They follow the generations before them and receive much guidance and nurture, but ultimately, they must run their own race.

Today, it is your turn on earth. Today, give God your heart. Today, lay hold of the opportunity to do God's will and give witness to the values of eternity. Today, rejoice to suffer the loss of all things so you may win Christ. Today, desire only that God may be glorified and enjoy God's blessings in this hour and all eternity. To the One who can put the imperishable on what is perishable, to him be honor and praise forever and ever.

Amen.

Living in God's Abundance

Matthew 6:25-33

After reading these words of scripture, the old Bobby McFerrin song gets stuck in my head: "Don't worry, be happy." Listening to that leads me to Bob Marley's song, "Don't worry about a thing, cause every little thing gonna be alright." On the surface, these songs seem to reiterate what Jesus is saying: Do not worry about your life or what you will eat, drink, or wear. Life is so much more than that. Consider the birds of the air and how they are fed. Consider the lilies of the field and how they grow and bring beauty. They are here one day and gone the next, but God takes care of them. How much more will God take care of you?

Worry, in the sense of being immobilized by fear and anxiety, will not add a single day to our lives, and it might take some days away. So, on the surface, this is good advice, but we know the teachings of Jesus are never quite that simple. When we scratch the surface and look deeper, this teaching yields profound insights and challenges.

First, this is not a lesson in laziness. God does work for good in our lives from an eternal perspective. God does take care of things, but that does not mean we don't have to study for the test or prepare for the presentation. If I haven't taken the time to prepare a sermon, then I should be worried standing in the pulpit. God wants us to be engaged in our own living. It is even okay to fret over how we might best deal with a crisis, conflict, or need. There is a type of worry or concern that motivates and is rooted in love. Jesus talks about something different here when he says, "Don't worry."

Jesus is certainly talking about something more than what we might call "first-world problems." Some of us should not worry about things like food and clothing. If you have a closet full of clothes and are still worried about what to wear, Wake up! You are wasting your life on lesser things, Jesus might say. If your all-consuming concern is whether to eat at this restaurant or that one, open your ears to the Spirit of the Lord saying, For goodness' sake, get over it. You are missing out on so much.

At the same time, for some, these are sincerely big concerns. For one who is truly concerned about food, shelter, and health care for themselves or those they love, we can't just say, "Don't worry." As we scratch the surface of this lesson, we see the deeper truth that we are actually called to enter into their concern. At the core, this lesson is about the kin-dom of God. Jesus says, "Strive first for the kingdom of God and God's righteousness (which, in Wesley's view, is always characterized by love), and all these things will be given to you as well." How does that work? Well, we start by realizing that the kin-dom of God is more than a place we go when we die. We are called to live in this beloved community now. We pray for God's will to be done on earth as it is in heaven. So, as we seek first God's will, we become the answer to the worries of others. We become the way things fall into place. We help decrease hunger, and worries about basic needs subside. If we see someone legitimately worried about food and shelter, we don't need to say, "Don't worry. Be happy." We ask ourselves, "What can I do?" That's seeking first to be a witness to God's blessed, beloved, and eternal community.

The United Methodist Church's *Book of Discipline* has a paragraph on how to fulfill our mission to make disciples of Jesus Christ. It says that we make disciples by seeking, welcoming, and gathering persons into the Body of Christ, by nurturing and equipping each other in Christian living, and also by sending "persons into the world to live lovingly and justly as servants of Christ by healing the sick, feeding the hungry, freeing the oppressed, and working to develop social structures that are consistent with the gospel."[11] That's how we seek first the ways of God.

We can't get there if we insist on seeing through the lens of scarcity, believing that there is not enough, and we must grab all we can and protect what we have. That is not kin-dom thinking. In God's providential care, there is enough food, clothing, care, and grace for everyone. With the words of this Sermon on the Mount, we are invited into God's abundance. When we enter into God's family, we enter into God's abundant love for all and become a part of distributing this abundance. We are called to cover the worries of the world.

John Wesley and the early Methodists tried to live this way, which is still in our spiritual DNA. Wesley talked a lot in his journals about what Methodists were doing to make a difference. In 1753, Wesley said, "I visited more of the poor sick. The industry of many of them surprised me. Several who were ill able to walk were nevertheless at work; some without any fire, bitterly cold as it was, and some, I doubt, without any food." "If you saw these things with your own eyes, how could you then lay out your resources in mere ornaments and selfish pursuits?" (Wesley uses the word "superfluities" here). That's a challenging question.[12]

In worship, we come together to receive the sacrament of Holy Communion. In this sacrament, we receive a piece of bread from a common loaf. Each of us only receives a small piece. No one gets it all. But together, this small piece connects us to something much bigger. In the sharing of this sacrament, we become a part of something larger than ourselves and larger than the elements before us. We find ourselves feasting from a table that extends into heaven itself. At this table, and in communion with God and one another, we can stop worrying about whether or not we are loved. We can receive the grace needed to lift another out of the darkness and into the light of God's love. And, in this sacrament, we know everything will be all right in God's eternal and providential care.

Amen.

Reflections for Devotion and Discipling

1. Within this sermon, Wesley asked this practical question worthy of our reflection: "What does it mean to serve God?" What does Jesus mean when he says we cannot worship both God and mammon?

   Serving God starts with faith, trusting in God as our source of strength and guidance. Once again, faith is more than believing. This faith leads to love for God and all creation. With faith, we are given a desire to reflect God's will on the world. That is how Wesley defines faith. Faith is our trust in God's love and always leads us into love.

2. How can we balance the two-edged calling here to not worry and to strive?

   Indeed, worry in the sense of being immobilized by fear will not add to our lives. At the same time, we are called to "strive" and "seek." We strive to be all God created us to be. As Wesley says, there is no place for sloth in true holiness. We seek not to establish our own righteousness but the righteousness of Christ. What does this look like?

3. How do we serve God as a congregation?

The Book of Discipline gives a wonderful blueprint for how a congregation fulfills the mission "to make disciples of Jesus Christ for the transformation of the world."

We proclaim the gospel. (This is at the top.)

We "seek, welcome, and gather persons into the Body of Christ." (This may sound obvious, but many congregations have an attitude of "we will welcome them if they come.")

We lead persons to commit their lives to God through baptism and professions of faith. (What processes are in place for this work?)

We nurture and equip persons in Christian living through worship, sacraments, spiritual disciplines, and other means of grace. (Do people even know what these words mean?)

We send persons into the world to live lovingly and justly as servants of Christ. (This is what happens outside the walls of the church.)

Continue to "seek, welcome, and gather." (This mission is cyclical and continuous. We can never say we are done.)

CHAPTER ELEVEN

"The Golden Rule"

Upon the Lord's Sermon on the Mount – Discourse 10

(A devotional paraphrase)

Sermon 30 in the Standard Sermons of John Wesley

Paraphrase of Wesley sermon

> *"Do not judge, so that you may not be judged. For the judgment you give will be the judgment you get, and the measure you give will be the measure you get.*
>
> **Matthew 7:1-12 – "The Golden Rule"**

Jesus starts a new section of his Sermon on the Mount with today's scripture. Having first summed up true religion and focusing on the relationship between intention and outward action, he now reveals some hindrances of this religion.

The first hindrance mentioned here is judging. There is no period of our life where this caution is not needed. The temptations are innumerable, with many so artfully disguised that we fall into the sin before we suspect any danger. The danger is great not only to those judged but to the one judging, wounding the soul, and exposing the judger to the judgment of God. As Paul says, when we judge others, we condemn ourselves because we do the same things. This act of judging divides and destroys in many ways.

Jesus asks, "Why do you see the speck in your neighbor's eye but do not notice the log in your own?" To fall into this trap is to notice the infirmities, mistakes, and weaknesses of others to avoid seeing such things in ourselves. To ignore our own "damnable impenitence," our own assured self-will, our own idolatrous love of the world is to make our whole lives "an abomination to the Lord." With such carelessness, we dance over the mouth of hell! The true follower of Christ always endeavors to be humble, gentle, merciful, and patient, even with what we deem evil. By the grace of God, we are called to spend our energy on self-examination rather than judgment.

But what is meant by the phrase "judge not"? It is not the same as speaking evil of another. Speaking in this way happens when one is absent. Judgment can happen in a person's presence. Likewise, judgment does not require speech at all. Even thinking of another in a manner contrary to love is the judgment that is here condemned. Judgment can manifest itself in many ways: by casting undeserved blame, by proclaiming guilt with no proof and thus committing slander, by questioning intent based on presuppositions that may not be true, or by insisting on our own way. Even our thinking in terms of judgment can create division and strife. How rarely would we fall into this trap of judging if we took seriously the counsel of our Lord to go to those we believe have trespassed and talk directly to them?

Now, suppose you, by the grace of God, have been able to remove the log from your eye and can see the speck or log in another's eye. To point this out can often make matters worse. If one is not ready to hear, such judgment can create a barrier rather than a bridge. Our zeal can lead them—and us—back into darkness. Therefore, let this hindrance of judgment be removed. Open your heart to God's love as it leads us to love others. In this movement, we discover the whole treasure of holiness and happiness.

Jesus follows this with some hard sayings that need some unpacking. He says, "Do not give what is holy to the dogs or cast your pearls to the pigs." As we seek to serve God, don't take love and turn it into self-righteous judgment. Don't take what is holy and turn it into something profane or divisive. And then, at a practical level, don't take the holy mysteries of God and try to give them to those who first need to know the basics: that God loves them and is there for them. Feed others with what is needed.

Be very careful about applying these sayings to other people. Be very reluctant to make this judgment about any other human being. Others may be so full of greed, anger, and love of the world that they will be unable to hear—and even turn against—those who try to share the good news.

Nevertheless, our calling is to share and to especially focus on the next exhortation: pray! To neglect this calling is another great hindrance to holiness. If all else fails in our efforts to share the good news with others, focus on this. Whatever you desire, as it connects to God's desires for us, "Ask and it shall be given; seek and you shall find; knock and it shall be opened to you."

Ask for what? To be who God calls you to be. "O how meek and gentle, how lowly in heart, how full of love for both God and humanity, might you have been on this day, if you had only asked—and continued in this prayer."

Next, seek! And do so in the way God has ordained for us: in searching the scriptures, hearing God's word, fasting, and partaking of the Lord's Supper. In this seeking, you will find. You will find that "pearl of great price," that faith that overcomes the world, that peace that the world cannot give, that love at the heart of our inheritance.

Knock, and the door of mercy, holiness, righteousness, and heaven shall be opened to you. Do not stop until this way is opened before you, and you can explore all the blessings of God's kingdom. The idea of persistence is implied in all three verbs: *continue asking*, *seeking*, and *knocking*. Be constant in the prayer that the compassion of our Lord will continually soften our hardened hearts and that we will continue to find "the love and the image of God."

Jesus proceeds to illustrate by pointing out how we give good things to our children when they ask. If a child asks for bread, we do not give a stone instead. If a child asks for fish, we don't give a snake. How much more then will God give us blessings of pure goodness? As explained in Luke's account of this story, God will give the Holy Spirit to us, which means all wisdom, peace, joy, love, and all the treasures of holiness and happiness. That's what comes to those who continually ask, seek, and knock.

Next, Jesus makes an important connection between prayer and how we treat others. We cannot expect to receive blessings from God while we fail to be charitable to our neighbors. We need to work at removing this barrier. Thus, Jesus immediately follows this word about prayer with the Golden Rule, the royal law of mercy and justice, a law which many believe to be engraved on the minds of everyone: "Do to others as you would have them do to you."

This rule can be understood in a positive or negative sense. In the negative sense, we don't like it when others judge us, causelessly think evil of us, or publish our faults and infirmities. So, don't do this to others. Positively, we hope others will respect us and behave towards us with justice, mercy, and truth. Let us live by this same rule. Let us love and honor all.

Do this and live! To truly love this way, we must understand it is all but impossible without the transforming love of God. We are able to love because God first loved us. Receiving the love of God empowers us to love our neighbor as ourselves. This transformation starts as the Holy Spirit reveals to each of us, in a personal way, that we are a beloved child of God. We open our hearts to this love and give our lives to it. That's faith. And then our faith begins to work for love. It becomes our joy to increase this love in the world. Seek after this love and faith and discover the life God wants for you and for all.

Amen.

Living Prayer (Preached on Back-to-School Sunday)

Matthew 7:1-12 and Ephesians 3:14-21

I am not good at sitting still and focusing on one thing for too long. I only half-jokingly say that one reason God called me into ministry is because God knew I couldn't sit in a pew for a whole hour. As I grew through school, I learned how to sit in class and enjoy it. My method was to actively take notes. This helped me a lot. But when it comes to worship and prayer, it is still hard for me. Profound, holy, life-giving thoughts get inside me, making me want to move. Sometimes, it is just more than I can take. I need to process it. And for me, that means physical movement is needed. While in the office, I get accused of pacing a lot.

This is one reason I think of exercise as a part of my prayer time. I have discovered that I can swim laps at the fitness center, run, or walk, and my racing mind empties all my immediate worries. I dedicate that open space in my heart to God. I don't try to fill that space with my words or desires for what I want God to do for me. I just swim or run and trust God is there, knowing God honors all those prayers racing through my mind and heart. Very often, in this open space, I am given a glimpse of God's advanced desires for me. And remember, that's what the word "prayer" means in the original language. A prayer is "an advanced desire." Praying is about moving from our petty, selfish desires into God's desires for us and for the world.

In our lesson, Jesus calls us to "suspend judgment." It's another way of saying, "Be open." In our natural state, our minds and hearts become so cluttered with judgment, and these judgments get in the way of God's transforming grace and guidance. Judgment blocks the light of God's love and can be so hurtful. For instance, a server spills a drink, and someone at the table rushes to judgment and calls them incompetent. I witnessed that recently. Or a politician says something, and they are immediately deemed "stupid."

A group of teachers recently did an experiment. One day, they all intentionally made some noticeable mistakes. One teacher messed up a simple equation. Another teacher wore mismatched shoes. Another forgot to shut their car door. Those are examples of some of the "mistakes." Then, these teachers listened closely to see how long it would take for students to publicly ridicule them, laugh at them, or spread rumors about them. It did not take long at all. The next day, the teachers gave their report, and hopefully, lessons were learned.

Jesus says, "Judge not." Judgment is not our responsibility. When we focus on the speck in another's eye and ignore the log in ours, we hurt others and ourselves. It is so easy for us to project our own shortcomings onto others when we judge them. Suspend judgment long enough to listen, long enough to see what is really going on beneath the surface, long enough to build a relationship. This is God's advanced desire for us.

In this lesson, we are again called to prayer: to ask, seek and knock. This is our constant work as we seek to grow in God's love. So, the question becomes, For what? What do we seek? We seek God's advance desires for us. We seek opportunities to be peacemakers. We seek ways to actively show love to those we know and especially to those we don't know, even those others might put down in some way. We have been challenged with such advanced desires throughout this series. In the Sermon on the Mount, we are called to put our prayers into action for others, actions that build community and make love come alive. Prayer does require movement.

Using Jesus' illustration, when we don't act upon our prayers this way, we take what is holy and throw it to the dogs. We profane the treasures of God when we store them only for selfish gain. We profane the holy love of God when we only think about what we want. God wants all that is good for us. This goodness is found as we open our hearts to others. God wants life-giving blessings for us. God wants the fruits of the spirit for us: love, joy, peace, patience, kindness, goodness, and the rest. As we say often, these blessings come to us on their way to someone else. They grow as they are shared. To hoard them or use them to manipulate things to our own ends is like taking what is holy and throwing it to the dogs, so to speak. It is to waste the gifts of God.

All this leads to the Golden Rule: "Do to others as you would have them do to you." Jesus calls this a summary of all the law and the prophets. And here is a good lesson about that. Jesus said the same about another key teaching. When Jesus talked about loving God with all of our heart, soul, mind, and strength and loving our neighbor as a part of ourselves, he also called that the summary of all the law and the prophets. So, there is a connection here. "Do unto others" and "love your neighbor as yourself" are two ways of saying the same thing. The bottom line is that we are called to actively love others. That's what we ask for. That's what we seek. That's what we do.

Yes, prayer requires movement. Prayer is meant to lead

us into love. So, I invite you to ask for real opportunities to give this witness. Pray daily. God might lead you to walk over to a new student or co-worker and say hello. You might be called to sit next to someone who others avoid. You might realize the person who hurt you is only human and needs to be forgiven. You might be given the courage to notice the log in your own eye and deal with it.

Here is my prayer for all of you, especially those in school. In addition to math, science, language arts, and social studies, I pray you will also comprehend the heights, depths, and breadth of God's love, as our first scripture lesson says. May God's love grow in your heart. That growth will happen as you get up, move, and actively seek God's will for you. Seek that growth and receive the blessings God wants for you.

Amen.

Reflections for Devotion and Discipling

1. What keeps us from fulfilling Jesus' call? What are some hindrances to true and life-giving faith?

The number one hindrance is judging. We are invited to suspend judgment and open ourselves to new possibilities in which the Spirit might move to transform us—not "them." How is judging harmful to others and our own souls? Why is it so tempting?

2. What do we ask for in prayer? What do we seek? On what door are we called to knock?

We "ask" to be who God calls us to be—meek, gentle, lowly in heart, full of love. This is to be our continuing prayer. We "seek" God's goodwill to be done through us. And we "knock" on the door that opens the way to holiness. What does this look like?

3. In this sermon, what is the connection between prayer and how we treat others?

We cannot expect blessings from God when we fail to be charitable, for example. We have said it often: God's love comes to us on its way to someone else. Prayer is a way that we open this flow.

4. How might we apply the Golden Rule? This rule can be applied negatively in terms of what not to do and positively in terms of what to do. What are some possibilities for both?

Jesus says this rule is a summary of all the law and the prophets. This makes it a key text by which we evaluate all scripture and whether the words are normative or descriptive for a particular time. This is the key principle of Wesleyan hermeneutics, as detailed more fully in another volume. Jesus said this same thing about other key teachings, specifically about loving God and our neighbor as ourselves. "Do unto others" and "Love your neighbor" can be seen as two ways of saying the same thing. With both, the call is to active love.

CHAPTER TWELVE

"The Narrow Way"

Upon the Lord's Sermon on the Mount – Discourse 11

(A devotional paraphrase)

Sermon 31 in the Standard Sermons of John Wesley

Paraphrase of Wesley sermon

> *"Enter through the narrow gate, for the gate is wide and the road is easy that leads to destruction, and there are many who take it. For the gate is narrow and the road is hard that leads to life, and there are few who find it."*
>
> **Matthew 7:13-14**

Jesus continues to warn of the dangers that plague our journey into true religion, both the hindrances that come from the sin within our hearts and those that come from beyond us. By these hindrances, many have fallen back into the darkness. So, for today, Jesus says, "Enter through the narrow gate. Wide is the gate, and broad is the road that leads to destruction. But small is the gate and narrow the road that leads to life." Yes, the way to darkness, dread, destruction, and death is the wide and broad way.

Root sins branch out and give rise to all others. The root sin is the carnal mind at odds with God; it is arrogance of heart, self-will, and love of the world. This root sin infuses itself into our every thought, infecting our every word and tainting all our actions. And the offspring of this root sin are more numerous than we can count in every age and nation.

To be clear, a part of this wide way is to look "over there," to look at Muslims, for example, or to place blame on those in the inner cities or those of other political persuasions. No. We only have to look among those who bear the name of Christ. Go no further than the communities to which we belong. There, all may seem well on the outside, but the inside is full of vanity, anger, covetousness, and lovers of pleasure more than God. We may be highly esteemed by others and still be an abomination to the Lord. We may practice the form of godliness outwardly but know little of inward holiness.

Along the wide way, we project all ills onto those who have less in terms of wealth, opportunity, or ambition. Often, the higher we rise in fortune and power, the deeper we sink into the wickedness of judging and dividing. We are tempted to use our honor and riches, learning and wisdom not as resources to help us grow in salvation but rather to excel in vice and ensure our own destruction. As Jesus wants us to see, this is the wide, easy, popular way, and it leads to narrowness of spirit.

Let us turn to the narrow way that leads to abundant and eternal life and the wideness of God's mercy. This way is so narrow that nothing unclean or unholy can enter. No sin can pass through this gate. The narrow way is the way of universal holiness. It is the way of poverty of spirit, holy mourning, and meekness; it is the way of mercy and purity of heart and the way that turns the other cheek and goes the extra mile. It is the way of all we have learned in this great Sermon on the Mount. Our calling as the church is to give witness to this way.

So many forces conspire to bring us into the wide way. There are many examples of the crude and rude side of life calling us to immediate pleasure and selfish indulgences that always leave us weaker than before. But there are also examples of polite and wise people who turn on anyone who makes them uncomfortable with their privilege. They speak in subtle ways that hurt or offend. They condemn evil but do not try to overcome it with good. It is hard for us to acknowledge this as the wide way precisely because it is bright, popular, easy, and big.

The typical method of persuasion for the wide way is not an appeal to understanding but to fear. This method has a high success rate because fear is easily taken in, whereas reasoning requires much more effort and a willingness to step into what is naturally uncomfortable and hard. Without a sure reliance on God's love, we fear questioning or challenging those who have the power of the world. We fall into the trap of believing their worldly success proves their righteousness. Worldly success becomes what we want. We defend those with worldly power, bow to them, and let them lead us along the wide way that destroys souls. If you dare to engage in honest self-examination, is this not so?

And then we are faced with the opposite way, the narrow way! It is uncomfortable and always calling us to change. In other words, striving for the narrow way means being in the minority. In addition, there is no way to argue for the narrow way, show its advantage in this world, or explain it rationally, even when we experience it. All our natural passions incline us to return to the broad way, the way of hate, division, winning, and greed.

In this context, our Lord gives this strong exhortation: strive to enter by the narrow gate. The Greek word *agonizomai* suggests "to agonize." Strive. Wrestle. Don't Settle. Agonize. The stakes are high. Later, Jesus will tell a parable of a master closing the door at the last possible moment and those standing outside begging for the door to be opened again. And the master says, "Depart, for you have chosen to be workers of iniquity" (Luke 13:24). Here, it seems the issue was their delay in seeking. Don't delay. We are invited into a sense of urgency when it comes to receiving the blessings of God in this life.

Therefore, strive now to enter by the narrow gate. See the wide way for what it is: the way that leads to division, destruction, and death. Examine your heart. Deep inside, you know the way of life. If you move just one step toward God, you are moving away from the pit of darkness and death. Strive to enter by the narrow gate. Be pierced with sorrow and shame for having so long run on the side of the unthinking crowd, utterly neglecting, if not despising, that "holiness without which no one can see the Lord." Strive by prayer, lifting up your heart to God, and giving God no rest until you awaken and grow in God's likeness. Strive by denying your own will and taking up your cross daily. Strive to make all your conversations instruments of healing rather than harm. In using the strongest metaphor from Jesus, be ready to cut off your right hand, pluck out your eye, and suffer the loss of goods, friends, health, and all things on earth so that you may enter the kingdom of heaven!

Amen.

The Wide Narrow Way

Matthew 7:13-14

I don't know about you, but it seems to me that the booths in restaurants keep getting smaller and narrower all the time. It's like someone comes in at night and squeezes them together. And I'll tell you, it makes me mad! Or have you been on an airplane lately? This one is not an illusion. Many airlines are squeezing the seats together to make room for more. If you are in a window or middle seat (God forbid) and you have to squeeze through, it can be very uncomfortable. Or what about a stadium, like War Memorial, where the numbers that mark the seats on the long benches are only inches apart? Narrow spaces can sometimes be impossible to navigate.

In religion, when we think of the narrow way, many see this through the lens of having to believe a particular way and affirm a specific, limited set of doctrines with just the right language. That's how we make it through. Often, this comes with a call to conform to a particular narrow image of what is deemed right and acceptable. This way of thinking can be attractive because it seduces us into an image of heaven where everyone is "like us." It is a comfortable thought to believe that the kingdom of God is this exclusive club and that "we" know the secret password to get in.

We must get beyond this constricted way of seeing the narrow way. I love where John Wesley speaks of the "narrowness of spirit." It is not a good thing. He used the phrase "narrowness of spirit" in the same sentence with bigotry and party zeal, with bigotry defined as "attachment to, or fondness for, our own party, opinion, church and religion." In this state, we forget that the word "party" is built on the word "part" and is not meant to be the whole. The narrow way is not about narrowing our spirits so that we are only comfortable in our own little world. John Wesley once said he would rather listen to a generous and kindhearted heathen than a Christian with a narrow soul.

When Jesus invites us through the narrow way, he is not inviting us to the "narrowness of spirit." In fact, he is inviting us into the opposite. As Wesley makes clear in his sermon on this passage, the wide and easy way is the way of division, contention, and judgment, all born out of deep fear. That's the way of the world. Along the wide way, we divide the world into "us" and "them." We think of scarcity as if there is only enough for some, and we want to ensure we are among those who have. Along the wide way, our spirits narrow, our hearts harden, and we focus on our own protection. In other words, the wide way of the world leads to narrowness of spirit.

On the other hand, the narrow way of Christ leads to wideness of spirit. We have been hearing about this way throughout this series. This narrow way leads to the blessings of being merciful and humble. It calls us into peacemaking and to love even our enemies. It is the way of God's abundance, where there is enough care, love, and resources for all. It is the way that leads us into the wideness of God's mercy, where we are not compelled to insist on our own way.

But make no mistake, this way is not easy. In fact, this narrow way can be downright uncomfortable for us, as illustrated in a story found later in the gospels where

Jesus speaks of a rich young man who wants to know what he needs to do to enter eternal life. Jesus enters into a conversation with this rich young man about the commandments. The man says he has kept them all. So, Jesus pushes him. "Then sell all you have," he says, "and give the money to the poor and follow me." This rich young man can't do it. Jesus turns to his disciples and says, "Truly I tell you, it is easier for a camel to go through the eye of a needle than for someone like this to enter the kingdom of God." The disciples were astounded. "Then who can be saved?" they asked. "If this person can't make it, who can?" This man is an insider. He has it all. Wealth. Youth. He is a man. He enjoys all the privileges that would have made them say he was truly blessed. At this point, Jesus looks at them and says, "For mortals it is impossible, but for God all things are possible" (Matt 19:16-25).

And that's the point. We don't make it into God's beloved community by our own merit. We make it—all of us—by the grace and power of God. We make it because love truly wins, even when we shut ourselves out. God opens and reopens the door, even into eternity. We make it because of God's abundant love. We make it because there is enough. It is a paradox. The narrow way—the way of Jesus—leads to life, abundant, eternal, wide, and full. The wide way of the world, the way of division, the way of protection, the way of building ourselves up over and against others leads to a dead-like existence. It leads to nothing.

"Strive," says Jesus, "to enter through the narrow gate." The Greek word here is a direct root of our English word "agonize." That's the call. It is not easy for us to enter into what is uncomfortable and hard. I think of the worship services where children help us pray together. We heard from some of them afterward that they were so nervous. It was hard for them to stand before the congregation and lead us in prayer, yet they did it, and their voices opened up the way for us to experience God's blessings. It was wonderful. That's an example of striving to enter by the narrow gate.

Reflecting on this text, I think of the classic poem "The Road Not Taken" by Robert Frost. Here is the last stanza: "I shall be telling this with a sigh, somewhere ages and ages hence: Two roads diverged in a wood, and I—I took the one less traveled by, and that has made all the difference."

Narrow souls follow the wide way of the world—allowing party zeal, impatience, judgment, bigotry, and bitterness to bring "disease" to the whole. Souls that are wide in love follow the narrow way, the "road less traveled," and it makes all the difference. Strive/agonize to enter God's kin-dom through the narrow way, through the way of God's wide and eternal love.

Amen.

Reflections for Devotion and Discipling

1. What is the paradox between the narrow and wide ways of the world? What are the challenges?

   Generally speaking, "narrow" is not favored. We like room—the more, the better. Ironically, many associate religion with a narrow set of beliefs and a particular approved way to express them. One attraction of this understanding is the way it lends itself to the idea that heaven is where everybody is "like us." As Jesus calls us to the narrow way, Wesley contrasts it with the term "narrowness of spirit." "Narrowness of spirit" is the way of prejudice, bigotry, and party zeal, as Wesley calls it. It is the opposite of Jesus' call to the narrow way. This narrow way is the harder way that leads us into the wideness of God's mercy. The wide and easy way of the world leads us into "narrowness of spirit." The narrow and hard way of love leads us into the "immeasurable riches of God's grace."

2. What spiritual commitments are needed to make it through the narrow way into the wideness of God's mercy?

   It is hard—if not impossible—for us, and that is the point. We cannot make it through on our own. "For mortals it is impossible, but for God all things are possible" (Matt 19:16-25). Living in this way requires the gifts of a faith that leads to love. It also calls us into a large and diverse community where we are able to practice the virtues of love.

3. What does it mean to "strive?"

As we have seen, the word "strive" means to agonize. We are not being called to something easy. What spiritual resources are needed to embrace the courage to agonize? What are some practical ways this might apply to you? What might you need to give up? What practices might you need to act upon?

4. In several of these sermons, Wesley makes his appeal by comparing and contrasting heaven and hell, the way of life and the way of destruction, and the wide and narrow way. What are deeper understandings of these terms and metaphors?

For Wesley, deliverance from hell involves more than simply believing. It involves a faith that works for love. Hell can be a present reality, giving a thousand times more pain than pleasure and always with the possibility of redemption. It is bigotry, party zeal, along with contention, revenge, malice, and other temperaments of the narrow way that can lead us into the "nethermost hell." Wesley was especially concerned with churches that become zealous in ways that drive each other into a state of division and schism. He says this can happen even when we "agree in essentials and only differ in opinions or in the circumstances of religion." The way to deliverance and "happiness" is love. Love is how we magnify the Lord and make true holiness known. If we try to hold to faith without this holiness and turn grace into an encouragement to sin, we can find ourselves again on the "way to the nethermost hell."

CHAPTER THIRTEEN

"True and False Prophets, Good and Evil Fruit"

Upon the Lord's Sermon on the Mount – Discourse 12
(A devotional paraphrase)

Sermon 32 in the Standard Sermons of John Wesley

Paraphrase of Wesley sermon

> "Beware of false prophets, who come to you in sheep's clothing but inwardly are ravenous wolves. You will know them by their fruits. Are grapes gathered from thorns or figs from thistles? In the same way, every good tree bears good fruit, but the bad tree bears bad fruit. A good tree cannot bear bad fruit, nor can a bad tree bear good fruit. Every tree that does not bear good fruit will be cut down and thrown into the fire. Thus you will know them by their fruits.
> **Matthew 7:15-20**

So many run to destruction and death because they will not be persuaded to walk in the narrow way. The lights of the easy, popular way shine so brightly, and people rush towards them. To warn against this deadly contagion, God has raised up prophets to point to the narrow way. But what if the leaders fall into the snare against which they warn others? What if their own prophecy deceives them? What if they lead others on the way of death and call it the way of life? How do we know?

Is this an uncommon thing? Sadly, it is not. We find it in every age. Therefore, our Lord includes this warning in his great sermon: "Beware of false prophets, who come to you in sheep's clothing but inwardly are ravenous wolves." First, remember that "prophet" means to "speak for God." Prophecy is not fortune-telling or predicting the future. Rather, it is a call to pursue the ways of God. Prophets teach the way of heaven as the narrow way. False prophets thus teach the wide way.

In the previous sermon, we learned that the narrow way is the way of humility, mourning, meekness, patience, doing good, and suffering evil. To teach any other way is to lead others into falsehood rather than truth, darkness rather than light, death rather than life. False prophets may use the good words of faith but twist them into the wide way that leads only to fear and death through the instruments of judgment, party zeal, unkindness to the neighbor or marginalized in our midst, and unconcern for good works. The wide way promotes narrowness of spirit.

Why would these false prophets teach this wide way? Because it is easy. It wins affection to tell people what they want to hear, encouraging their pride and passions, excusing harmful and unkind ways, and preaching an easy forgiveness and cheap grace. That is the false and wide way.

As Jesus says, false prophets tend to come as wolves in sheep's clothing. On the outside, they appear harmless. They elicit trust and seem to do good. They make you believe they have your best interest at heart—and they might even believe this. False prophets are likely to come with the "appearance of religion." They claim to have God's backing, all out of love for you. They may use the right language—faith, blessings, love, the middle way of kindness and temperance—but all to keep you dependent and focused on their view of righteousness.

Our Lord gives us a plain rule for discerning a false prophet in our midst: "You shall know them by their fruits." First of all, what is the fruit in their own lives? Are they focused on getting attention and cultivating their image, or do they illuminate the image of God? Are they meek and merciful? Do they promote peacemaking? Do they bear the fruits of the Spirit and cultivate these fruits in the lives of others? If not, it is manifest proof that God has not sent them. True prophets bring the proud, the passionate, and the unmerciful into the transforming grace of God, where they become humble and kind, focused on sharing the love of God with all, with less judgment and more compassion. They bear the good fruits of holiness.

False prophets, on the other hand, destroy and devour the flock for their own gain. They divide with self-righteousness and are passionate about maintaining the purity of their perspective. The fruits come from division, self-righteousness, and fear—all in the name of holiness.

So, we must ask, what if we think we are being deceived by a false teacher? How do we make the judgment without falling into the same trap? Do we continue to go to church and listen to them or not? My first inclination is to tell you to avoid them, but on deeper reflection, I read where Jesus talks about the Scribes and Pharisees who sit in Moses' seat and teach the people. Jesus tells the people to listen to the word of God in what they say and to follow it, even if they "say but don't do" (see Matt 23:1-3). In our day, these same teachers may be ordained to administer the sacrament of

Holy Communion. If I were to direct people away from the churches they serve, I might be, in effect, cutting them off from this ordinance of God. I dare not do this. The validity of the sacrament does not depend on the goodness of the one administering it but only on the faithfulness of the one who ordained it.

Thus, my counsel is to wait upon God by humble and earnest prayer and then act according to your best light. In this action, take care that you do not judge rashly or do not lightly think of anyone as a false prophet. If they challenge or make you uncomfortable, that may be a sign of their true calling from God. If they are leading the church into judgment rather than mercy, division rather than peace, and self-righteousness rather than lifting up the love of Christ, then you have cause for concern. Even then, however, make sure there is no anger or contempt in your heart. You may quietly seek out another who will help you grow in spiritual health. Or, for the sake of the church, you may stick it out, deciding this leader might even make you stronger by motivating you to more reflection and study. If you do continue to listen to them, be cautious. Hear with fear and trembling lest you be deceived and be tempted by their strong delusion.

I cannot conclude without addressing those of whom we speak. To all false prophets, pastors, priests, and preachers, hear the word of the Lord. How long will you lie in the name of God? How long will you pervert the right ways of the Lord, putting darkness for light? How long will you teach the ways of death and call it the way of life? Have you so given into the delusion that you actually believe it? Can you not see the fruits you are producing?

Dear colleagues, open your eyes before it is too late. Humble yourself before God. Cry out to God out of the dust that God may awaken your soul and give you the faith that works by love, the faith that is lowly and meek, pure and merciful, and zealous for good works. May the word of the Lord be a hammer that breaks the hardened heart and opens the way for God's true blessings. Having then, by God's grace, turned many to righteousness, may you "shine as the stars for ever and ever."

Amen.

Hearing Prophets

Matthew 7:15-20

Not long ago, I visited Duke Divinity School, the seminary I attended. It was a great experience to walk through those halls again. But I've got to tell you, there was something profoundly solemn about it as well. It wasn't sad, but it was solemn and even sobering. It didn't take me long to notice that new rooms and buildings were named after some of my professors who are no longer with us. I walked into Goodson Chapel, for example. It is a beautiful new chapel named after Bishop Goodson, who taught my first class in Methodism. Next, I almost cried when I walked into Langford Memorial Hall. Tom Langford had a huge impact on my life. I was reminded that time marches on, and to use an image from scripture, the "grass withers and the flowers fade." Our time comes and goes. Life has a way of making room for new acts of beauty, new opportunities for leadership, and new voices to be heard.

To put it more directly, I had a spiritual moment when I was able to face the truth that life is not about me. I am a part of something so much bigger. Sometimes, I wish I could freeze time and keep things the way I would like them to be, but that is not possible. I am dust, as the scripture says, and to dust, I shall return. At the same time—and this is big—I am a child of God, and I know the One who does have the power to give new and eternal life, the One who truly wants to include me in this glorious march through time and space, and who tells me that nothing, in life or in death, can separate me from the love of God through Christ Jesus our Lord.

Now, this is a hard, yet deeply spiritual, insight to recognize and accept. There is a connection between our realizing that we are finite and limited on one hand but given the gifts of God's eternal life and love on the other. It is hard for us to allow ourselves to be embraced by God when we are so busy trying to hang on and make it on our own.

I have learned this lesson from good prophets in my life. In the scriptures, a prophet is simply one called and empowered to "speak for God." The struggle for us is distinguishing between a true prophet and a false prophet. In our lesson, Jesus gives us a straightforward way to make this determination. He says it twice: "We will know them by their fruits."

We don't have to be geniuses to know what kind of fruit Jesus is talking about. He has laid it out in this sermon from the mountain. We have been hearing about this fruit throughout this whole series. Blessed are the humble.

Blessed are the merciful. Blessed are those who hunger for God's righteousness, justice, and love. Blessed are peacemakers. Love your enemies. Go the extra mile to show someone the patient, kind, and humble love of God. That's the fruit of a true prophet.

So, how might we characterize a false prophet? False prophets focus on judgment and project evil onto others rather than call people to look in the mirror. False prophets try to hang on to power rather than share it with others. False prophets promote division and see themselves as the righteous ones. False prophets tend to confirm our ways to keep our support and fail to acknowledge that God's ways are not our ways (see Isa 55:8).

Now, I've been talking a lot about others so far. If I take this whole Sermon on the Mount seriously, I've got to know that every part is a call not just to look out there but also inside me. This admittedly brings some fear and trembling to my heart. I like getting paid. I want you to like me. I like seeing my name listed as pastor. I can find biblical support for that as well. Communities need pastors. That is important. But is it possible to be a pastor and neglect a prophetic call or neglect to share God's challenging word? We tend to associate being a pastor with the care and comfort of others while being a prophet means speaking words that call for transformation. A false prophet might lean too far to the pastoral side, simply comforting and caring without calling people to practice true holiness.

Hear this tale of two kings and their prophets from the scriptures. First is King Ahab, who wants to go to war, so he asks his "advisors" or "prophets" about it. Most of these advisors or prophets tended to affirm what they believed the king wanted. However, one prophet in King Ahab's court was different. His name was Micaiah, and King Ahab says this about him: "I hate him … because he never prophesies anything good concerning me." That is a haunting line. In the scriptures, other prophets beg Micaiah to go along, but his sense of integrity and calling would not allow it (see 1 Kings 22).

The other example is King David and his prophet Nathan. King David had been the type of person who could fall into the mud and come up smelling like a rose every time. Everything seemed to go his way. But then, he took all this for granted, believing he could get away with anything. To make a long story short, he ended up having an affair with Bathsheba and even found a way to permanently get rid of Uriah, Bathsheba's husband. King David thought he had escaped another predicament, but one of his prophets, Nathan, confronted him with great fear and trembling. It is a great story to read. To his credit, David listens and repents. He calls out to God for mercy and to create in him a clean heart (see 2 Sam 12 and Ps 51).

These prophets are known to us not because they wanted to make a name for themselves but because they had God's word in them and had the courage to share it. I hope I am able to do that when God calls. I trust God will give you that opportunity as well. How will you respond?

Amen.

Reflections for Devotion and Discipling

1. How is the word "prophet" defined? What is the call and challenge of a true prophet as opposed to a false prophet?

   The wide and easy way is so tempting. To warn and guide us into the way of life, God raises up prophets, those who "speak for God." There are many, however, who make this claim. Therefore, we need to discern who is a true prophet and who is a false prophet. To do so, we must immerse ourselves in this whole Sermon on the Mount.

2. If we determine in our hearts that a pastor, for example, is leading us astray, is this a reason to stop going to that church or refrain from listening to them? What is Wesley's counsel?

   The answer to this question is complicated. How can staying keep us from falling into the trap of judging and help us understand more clearly what we should do? What might the sacrament of Holy Communion have to do with this decision? Is it important to stay within the larger church?

3. What are the differences and complementary characteristics of a pastor and a prophet? Is balance needed? Read the stories of Micaiah (1 Kings 22:1-35) and Nathan (2 Sam 12; Ps 51). What do they model for us?

Communities need pastors to share prophetic words and prophets who are pastoral. Why is this balance important? What are the challenges?

CHAPTER FOURTEEN

"Building on Solid Rock"

Upon the Lord's Sermon on the Mount – Discourse 13

(A devotional paraphrase)

Sermon 33 in the Standard Sermons of John Wesley

Paraphrase of Wesley sermon

"Not everyone who says to me, 'Lord, Lord,' will enter the kingdom of heaven, but only the one who does the will of my Father in heaven. On that day many will say to me, 'Lord, Lord, did we not prophesy in your name, and cast out demons in your name, and do many mighty works in your name?' Then I will declare to them, 'I never knew you; go away from me, you who behave lawlessly.'"

"Everyone, then, who hears these words of mine and acts on them will be like a wise man who built his house on rock. The rain fell, the floods came, and the winds blew and beat on that house, but it did not fall because it had been founded on rock. And everyone who hears these words of mine and does not act on them will be like a foolish man who built his house on sand. The rain fell, and the floods came, and the winds blew and beat against that house, and it fell—and great was its fall!"

Matthew 7:21-27

In the great Sermon on the Mount, Jesus has led us into the core teachings for the children of God, and now he closes with these weighty words. In this conclusion to the series, we will consider what it means to build our spiritual house either upon sand or rock.

Those who are foolish build their spiritual house on sand. This metaphor is used for those who hear God's word but do not practice it. Jesus elaborates by saying, "Not everyone who calls me Lord shall enter the kingdom, but only those who do the will of my Father in heaven." We cannot think of going to heaven by any other way than the way Jesus has just described. We certainly cannot think we will enter the kingdom by "verbal religion," which includes all creeds and prayers we may repeat. We may speak good of God and declare his love. We may be able to—or think we can—explain all the mysteries of God's kingdom. We may speak with the tongues of angels. And still, all this may be no more than saying, "Lord, Lord." I may successfully preach to others, lead many to salvation, and still be a castaway. I may bring many to the kingdom of God, but my words, in themselves, will not bring me into the kingdom.

Likewise, we may practice the principle of "do no harm." We may abstain from every outward wickedness and still not be justified. We may also engage in many good works. We may attend the Lord's Supper, search the scriptures regularly, hear an abundance of sermons, do good to our neighbor, feed the hungry, and still have no part in the glory of God. These blessings can set our face toward heaven, but alone, they are nothing. If not means to faith, mercy, and love of God, they are tools for building on sand.

If this shocks you, then you may need to entertain the

thought that you are a stranger to the whole religion of Jesus Christ. As clearly as possible, Jesus says we cannot enter the kingdom of heaven without this kingdom at work within us. Yes, many will come to me on that day, says Jesus, and talk about all the prayers they have said, and how they refrained from doing evil, and how they did good works and were not like others, and Christ may still say, You cannot enter until your heart is right, until the image of God is renewed within you. Everyone who relies on their own righteousness, good works, and religion is like one who builds a house on sand. The rains descend, the floods come, the wind blows, and the house falls. The storms of arrogance, anger, fear, judgment, and desire will be too great to withstand.

In contrast, the wise build their spiritual home on the rock. Drawing from the well of Jesus' Sermon on the Mount, the wise are the poor in spirit, who know they do not have the resources to give life to themselves. They are aware of their sin and guilt and of the perfect love of Christ demonstrated and given on the cross. They desire to be peacemakers, and with the peace and joy of the Holy Spirit, their wisdom is marked by humility, gentleness, and patience to all, never "returning evil for evil." They hunger and thirst for nothing on earth but only for the living God. They are filled with the love of God for all and even willing—because they see through the lens of eternity—to love their enemies. They see that the purpose of humankind is to glorify God, love God, and enjoy God's blessings forever. On this rock, we are justified by grace through the redemption in Christ Jesus and the life we now live; we live by faith in him, who loves us and gave himself for us (Gal 2:20).

Yet, let no one think this life with God shields us from the storms of temptation. These storms may even be more severe because we know Christ. The floods will come. The wind will blow. But they can't prevail over this foundation. Those who build on Christ by faith and love shall not be torn down.

Each of us must apply these words to ourselves, examining the foundation on which we are building our lives. Rock or sand? Are you building on "orthodoxy, or right opinions, which, by a gross abuse of words, I have called faith?" It is madness to build on such opinions, supposing that we are more scriptural than others and using scripture to divide and bring harm. We may belong to the best church with the purest doctrine and the most biblical form of government in our estimation, but if we build our faith upon this set of beliefs and opinions, we are building on sand or "on the froth of the sea!"

Therefore, build upon the rock. By the grace of God, know yourself. See yourselves as "poor in spirit." Then, add the meekness that allows you to be gentle and patient with others. Hunger and thirst are not for meat that perishes but for that which endures to eternal life. Focus not on the riches, honors, and pleasures of the world. And beware of trying to quench this hunger with what is vulgarly called religion—that poor, dull farce of outward show, which leaves the heart still cleaving to the dust. Let nothing satisfy you but the dwelling of God within.

Knowing you can do all things through Christ who strengthens you, be merciful as God is merciful. Love your neighbor as a part of yourself. Let this love be "kind, soft, benign, inspiring you with the most amiable sweetness, and the most fervent and tender affection." Cover all things in this love that hopes all things, endures all things, and never fails in time or in eternity.

Next, be pure in heart, purified through faith from every unholy affection—from pride, from anger, from every unkind and turbulent passion—by meekness and mercifulness. Let your religion be a religion of the heart, a heart filled with grace and peace towards all people, while at the same time, hungry for the living God, longing to grow in God's likeness. That's what it means to build upon the rock. It is to see this whole Sermon on the Mount as your resource and motivation. The wise ones build their home upon this rock.

Amen.

Doing What You Know

Matthew 7:24-27

I invite you to revisit your childhood dreams about what you wanted to be growing up. My guess is that you had some big dreams. You dreamed of things beyond ordinary or average. In late elementary school, I dreamed of being a wide receiver for the Razorbacks. I worked at it. I was well on my way (or at least I like to think I was), and then in the ninth grade, two days before school started, I broke my left shoulder for the second time. After this second break, one week before school started, I quit football, joined the band, and then began to dream of becoming a rock star someday.

I hope you still dream of being great in the context

of your life—being a great spouse, parent, employer, or employee. I hope you dream of being a great example of faith, hope, and love. It is good to dream big about such things.

In the Sermon on the Mount, found in Matthew Chapters 5-7, Jesus challenges us to rise above what is ordinary. "An eye for an eye," for example, was the law, the baseline, the general expectation. Jesus calls his disciples to something beyond this average. We don't retaliate in this way. We ask, how can we respond in a life-giving way that honors the way of forgiveness, mercy, and love?

Jesus then says, "You have heard it said, 'Love your neighbor' but I say to you 'Love your enemy as well.'" What good does it do to only love those you know will love you back or only spend time with people you like? That's average. We are called to something more. We are called to be those who try to honor and seek relationships with those who are different from us, even our enemies.

In our lesson today, Jesus continues to illustrate how to excel beyond what is ordinary. He explains there are two kinds of people when it comes to hearing the word of God: those who hear it and know what they should do but fail to do it and those who know what they should do and do something about it. This second way is lifted up as the model. We are called to "do what we know." Think about marriage, for example. We know we need to listen attentively and lovingly. We know we need to find ways to make our spouse feel special and loved. The question is, are we doing what we know we need to do? People who aspire beyond what is ordinary act on what they know.

When it comes to church, the average is to attend. We show up. But the challenge is to do something about it, to allow our presence to change us in some way. Hopefully, for all of us, there are times when the connection is made, and we start to act upon the blessings that have been given. That's what God wants for us as we attend to the means of grace—worship, prayer, Bible study, and the like.

Jesus continues his illustration by giving us a positive and negative image. He looks upon the crowd and says, "All of you have heard the word of God, yet some of you will be wise about it and some foolish. What's the difference? Listen to this passage again (v. 24): "Everyone who hears these words of mine" and what? (Understands them, no; takes notes on them, no; repeats them on social media, no). "Everyone who hears these words of mine and *acts on them* will be like a wise person who builds a house on rock." A major key to a life beyond the ordinary or typical is to put the words of Jesus into practice.

Jesus goes on to say, "The rains fell, the floods came, and the winds blew, but the house did not fall because it had been founded on rock." It is important for us to note that storms will come. Jesus is not teaching us how to avoid the storms. Faith will not make the storms detour around us, at least not every time. The good news is that we can endure the storms. We can build a foundation so it can handle any storm this world throws at us. We can intentionally build a life on the virtues of love and forgiveness, faith and grace. We can intentionally put into practice a life lived from an eternal perspective, knowing we are a part of something so much bigger than ourselves. And then, when the storms come, our spiritual home will stand.

In the sermon from Wesley, which inspired this devotion, we get a great summary of how salvation works.

It starts with a sense of humility, where we recognize our own sinfulness and our deserving of "hell" itself. This humility opens the way to God's amazing grace, which comes through the redemption in Christ Jesus our Lord. This redemption, in turn, opens the way to a life of love, a heavenly life lived now, where we grow in holiness, defined through the virtues of love, and are able to glorify, or magnify, the Lord. If we try to hold to faith without this holiness and turn grace into an encouragement to sin, we can find ourselves again building on sand.

Here is the bottom line. Average people know what to do. Those who excel beyond this point *do what they know*. And knowing is not about having some sign written in the sky or a lightning-bolt revelation. You have already heard God's word. You can name the virtues you are called to practice daily. You already know what to do. Maybe today is the day you pick one of these virtues named throughout this series and act upon it. When it comes to how we love and forgive, treat others, and take care of ourselves, we are all called to something more than what is ordinary, typical, or average. The Sermon on the Mounts sets the bar high.

Amen.

Reflections for Devotion and Discipling

1. According to Jesus and Wesley's interpretation, what does building your spiritual home on sand look like? What does this metaphor convey?

   We conclude the Sermon on the Mount with a word about building on rock. Jesus juxtaposes this with building on sand. As Wesley illuminates, the danger comes when we fail to act or begin to believe that religion is about verbal assent to a set of doctrines. An even greater danger is believing that faith is about defending our views. While Wesley held the church's creeds, articles, and homilies in his heart and saw them as a means to shape his life, he repeatedly used the word "orthodoxy" to describe this great spiritual sin. Building faith on the belief that our opinion is "right" and that our calling is to defend our beliefs is not only to build our spiritual home on sand but also to build on the "froth of the sea."

2. What does it mean to build your spiritual home on the rock? What does this metaphor convey? How is Christ to be understood as the rock?

   To understand what it means to build on rock requires a review of the whole Sermon on the Mount. This is the conclusion and, thus, a wrap-up. Those who build on the rock know they are "poor in spirit." They know they do not have the resources to give life to themselves. Those who build on the rock are peacemakers; they strive/agonize for the kin-dom of God; they intentionally love those who others might call enemies. These are examples of the shocking and counter-cultural characteristics of those who build on the rock. At another level, we believe Christ is the rock. Our relationship with Christ empowers us to stand through all storms. As we build, we are transformed into the image of Christ, from one degree to another (2 Cor 3:18).

3. Continuing this thought, what does our transformation look like? How are we able to participate in our own transformation?

In this larger series, we have explored the difference between change and transformation. Change is doing something in a different way. Transformation is becoming something new. For example, a change is to go for a run instead of our usual walk; a transformation is to become a runner. We are called to grow into who we are in God's eyes, so to speak. We are new creations in Christ. We are the light of the world and the salt of the earth. We have been transformed. While transformation comes from God, as Wesleyans, we believe we are called to participate in our own growth, from babes to maturity. In change, we tend to add things to our lives. We say, "I need to do this or that." The way of transformation is opened more fully by "letting go." Wesley interprets "purity of heart" in this vein; we purify or clear the way for God to move in and through us. Building on Jesus' sermon, Wesley calls us to let go of our worldly treasure hunt so we might store up treasures in heaven. We let go of our judgment, anger, greed, lust, and self-righteousness, among other dispositions that bring harm and hurt into the world. We build on the rock by letting go of the self-deception that we can handle it all on our own. By letting go and letting God in, we are transformed in the image of Christ. As Wesleyans, we are optimistic about this possibility. This whole Sermon on the Mount moves us in this direction.

About the Authors

Michael Roberts is the senior pastor at First United Methodist Church in Jonesboro, Arkansas, and previously served at First United Methodist Church in Conway, Arkansas, where this series began to take shape. He holds degrees from the University of Central Arkansas (B.A.), Duke University Divinity School (M.Div.), and Southern Methodist University (D.Min.). He has served on the Cabinet as the Director of the Restart Initiative and as the Director of Connected In Christ, an intentional leadership and congregational development process designed to "facilitate the connections needed for faithful and fruitful ministry." He also serves on the General Conference delegation for the Arkansas Conference. His wife, Dede, is also an ordained United Methodist pastor, and they have three children, all adults, and two grandchildren.

Lauren DeLano Grosskopf is the associate pastor at First United Methodist Church in Russellville, Arkansas, and previously served as the pastor at Vilonia United Methodist Church and with Michael at First United Methodist Church in Conway, Arkansas. She holds degrees from Hendrix College (B.A.) and Boston School of Theology, Boston University (M.Div.). She also serves on the Jurisdictional Conference delegation. Her husband, Dr. Jacob Grosskopf, is an associate professor of geology at Arkansas Tech University.

Endnotes

1. Howard A. Snyder, *The Radical Wesley, The Patterns and Practices of a Movement Maker* (Seedbed, 2014), Kindle 845. He says, "Wesley was very clear that salvation was wholly by grace alone. But he was equally insistent that God graciously enabled men and women to cooperate with the Holy Spirit in the great work of salvation, of restoring the image of God."

2. For a gracious and good account of this optimism and how it compares with other popular perspectives, see Don Thorsen, *Calvin vs. Wesley: Bringing Belief in Line with Practice* (Abingdon Press, 2013).

3. Paul W. Chilcote, *Multiplying Love: A Vision of United Methodist Life Together* (Abingdon Press, 2023), 60, and Paul W. Chilcote, *Recapturing the Wesleys' Vision: An Introduction to the Faith of John and Charles Wesley* (IVP Academic, 2009), 27. "Faith is a means to love's end ... Faith without activated love (on the one hand) and works founded upon anything other than God's grace (on the other hand) are equally deficient visions of the Christian life."

4. Ted Campbell, *Methodist Doctrine: The Essentials, 2nd ed.* (Abingdon Press, 2012), 59f. Wesley wanted to illuminate the "process by which women and men actually live out the life of grace." As "first order theology," Wesley's sermons (along with his Notes on the Bible, Liturgies, and Prayers) illuminate this "way of salvation." Also see Richard Heitzenrater, *Wesley and the People Called Methodists* (Abingdon Press, 2013). Within is a good account of Wesley offering these sermons to provide homiletical boundaries, especially for the unordained and lay preachers within the movement, similar to the Book of Homilies found in the Anglican tradition. Also see Thomas A. Langford, *Practical Divinity: Theology in the Wesleyan Tradition* (Abingdon Press, 1983), 25. The scriptures convey the knowledge of God "as its words are transposed to experience by the Holy Spirit." These sermons as doctrine are meant to facilitate this movement.

5. The reordering of Wesley's sermons to fit within the liturgical year is unique to this series and is offered as a way to bring these teachings to life in a new way. The first volume is entitled *Wanting More: Advent, Christmas, and Epiphany, Inspired by the Teachings of John Wesley*. This book starts with Wesley's sermon "The Means of Grace" and "Circumcision of the Heart," and includes others. The series for Epiphany highlights the first eight sermons in the Standard Sermons. These sermons are foundational, which is the reason they are first. A forthcoming volume will focus on Lent, Easter, and Pentecost, building upon Wesley's sermons entitled "The Wilderness State," "Manifold Temptation," "Self-Denial," and "Original Sin," among others. The series for Easter will be built on the sermons entitled "New Birth," "Marks of a New Birth," and "The Great Privilege of Those Who are Born of God," with a series leading up to Pentecost using the sermons entitled "The Lord Our Righteousness," "The Witness of the Spirit," "The Witness of Our Own Spirit," and "The Spirit of Bondage and Adoption." For the second half of Ordinary Time, there will be a volume on discipleship, stewardship, and spiritual growth, building upon multiple sermons including "On Schism," "A Caution Against Bigotry," "Catholic Spirit," "Sin in Believers," "Cure for Evil Speaking," "Use of Money," "The More Excellent Way," and "Christian Perfection."

6   Forty-four sermons are officially named as Standard Sermons and are part of our doctrine. Many other sermons were published, some of which have been considered within the Standard Sermons at times, even by Wesley himself. Many are historical favorites and provide great insights into the understanding and practice of faith, even as they reveal change and growth in Wesley's own theological thought. I have been able to use these sermons as the basis for a class with some of the lectures developed into a video series entitled "A Graceful Way – Methodist History and Doctrine" (found on YouTube @michaelroberts3091). There are twelve videos, published during the pandemic, including "Wesley Who?," "Epworth to Aldersgate," "The Birth of a Church," "True Religion," "Scriptural Holiness," "Wesley and Calvin," "The Way of Salvation," and "The Via Media," Michael Roberts, 2021.

7   Ashley Boggan D, *"The Wesleys' Enduring Message,"* United Methodist Communications, August 2022 (a podcast with transcript).

"John and Charles Wesley were God-loving agitators and Spirit-filled dissidents. They knew how to find a line, walk right up to that line and then jump right over it." Here Dr. Boggan explores the history of "consenting to be more vile" in Bristol, following George Whitfield's lead. After being criticized and threatened for move, Wesley defended himself and other preachers with the phrase, "The world is my parish." In this context, the world is not seen as the globe but as one step outside the church.

See also Ashley Boggan D, *"Wesleyan Vile-tality: A Call to Reclaim Our Wesleyan Heritage,"* Arkansas Conference, arumc.org., 2023. Also see Ashley Boggan D., Wesleyan Vile-tality, Methodist History, (Vol. 61, No. 1, 2023, Scholarly Publishing Collective: A Duke University Press Initiative). In this important lecture, Dr. Boggan uses the coined word "vile-tality" to explore ways in which we might reclaim our calling to spread the love of God to as many people as possible. Wesley consented to be "more vile" in his decision to proclaim the gospel outside the walls of the church and meet people where they were, using language that would be relevant and understandable. This was a major turning point for the movement. And it doesn't end with Wesley. For another example, one of the first female preachers within the movement, Mary Fletcher Bosanquet, said: "I am conscious how ridiculous I must appear in the eyes of many ... I do nothing but what Mr. Wesley approves, and as to the reproach thrown by some on me, what have I to do with it, but quietly go forward saying, 'I will still be more vile, if my Lord requires it.'" "It's four o'clock somewhere." If you know, you know.

8   William H. Willimon, *Remember Who You Are: Baptism, a Model for Christian Life (The Upper Room Press, 1998) 29.*

9   This idea was inspired by a sermon and video from Northpoint Church entitled "Anything but Average," found at northpoint.org., 2015. The idea was used in the fourteenth sermon of this series as well.

10 More liberties have been taken with this introduction than normal, but the way Wesley begins this sermon, along with its repeating theme, sparked these thoughts.

11 *Book of Discipline of the United Methodist Church* (United Methodist Publishing House, 2016), ¶122.

12 For a powerful account of Wesley's heart for the poor and marginalized, see Theodore W. Jennings, *Good News to the Poor: John Wesley's Evangelical Economics* (Abingdon Press, 1990).

www.ingramcontent.com/pod-product-compliance
Lightning Source LLC
Chambersburg PA
CBHW070539170426
43200CB00011B/2481